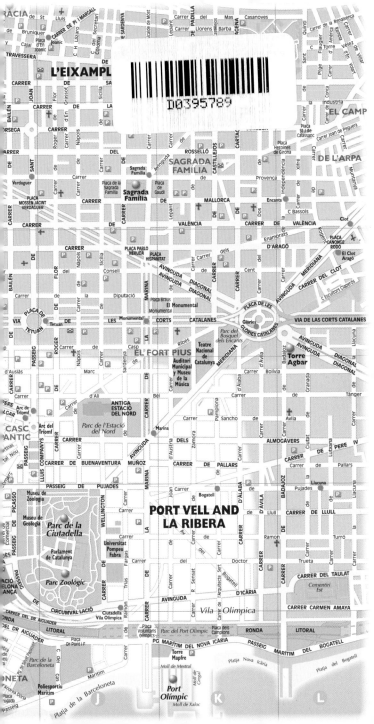

2

Barcelona's
25Best

by Michael Ivory

Fodor's Travel Publications
New York • Toronto •
London • Sydney • Auckland
www.fodors.com

How to Use This Book

KEY TO SYMBOLS

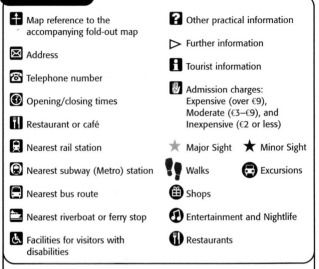

- 🔲 Map reference to the accompanying fold-out map
- ✉ Address
- ☎ Telephone number
- 🕐 Opening/closing times
- 🍴 Restaurant or café
- 🚆 Nearest rail station
- Ⓜ Nearest subway (Metro) station
- 🚌 Nearest bus route
- ⛴ Nearest riverboat or ferry stop
- ♿ Facilities for visitors with disabilities

- ❓ Other practical information
- ▷ Further information
- ℹ Tourist information
- ✋ Admission charges: Expensive (over €9), Moderate (€3–€9), and Inexpensive (€2 or less)
- ★ Major Sight   ★ Minor Sight
- 👣 Walks   🚍 Excursions
- 🎁 Shops
- 🎵 Entertainment and Nightlife
- 🍴 Restaurants

This guide is divided into four sections

- Essential Barcelona: An introduction to the city and tips on making the most of your stay.
- Barcelona by Area: We've broken the city into five areas, and recommended the best sights, shops, entertainment venues, nightlife and restaurants in each one. Suggested walks help you to explore on foot.
- Where to Stay: The best hotels, whether you're looking for luxury, budget or something in between.
- Need to Know: The info you need to make your trip run smoothly, including getting about by public transport, weather tips, emergency phone numbers and useful websites.

Navigation In the Barcelona by Area chapter, we've given each area its own colour, which is also used on the locator maps throughout the book and the map on the inside front cover.

Maps The fold-out map accompanying this book is a comprehensive street plan of Barcelona. The grid on this fold-out map is the same as the grid on the locator maps within the book. We've given grid references within the book for each sight and listing.

Contents

CONTENTS

Introducing Barcelona

Self-confident, prosperous and buzzing Barcelona, capital of the autonomous Spanish region of Catalonia, is one of Europe's most compelling cities, pulling in millions of annual visitors who flock here to experience its style and diversity.

So, what's it got? The answer is something for everyone: stunning architecture, fine museums, excellent shopping, some inspirational food, and great cafés and nightlife. Not to mention the bonus of the city's seafront position, its medieval core, spacious boulevards and surrounding green hills.

The last decades have seen immense social, cultural and economic changes, with the physical reality of the city being changed by vast and ongoing building projects and Barcelona's role as Catalan capital becoming increasingly important. Economically, local industry contributes a good percentage of Spain's overall output, coining in the profits to both the private and public sector. The powers-that-be spend the money relatively wisely, with the innovative 'Barcelona Model', where public and private spending are seamlessly mixed, hailed by urban planners everywhere. The flip side of this regeneration has been the dramatic rise in the cost of housing, with prices increasing by more than 60 per cent in the last few years. Young couples are now being forced out to the sprawling satellite settlements. This is putting pressure on small city businesses, with traditional shops being replaced by tourist-friendly outlets.

Since the 1960s the city has seen a huge influx of immigrants, both from other parts of Spain and from North Africa and South America. Assimilation has progressed relatively smoothly, though it's been an effort for a small city that has until recently struggled itself to keep its Catalan identity. Factors like these make Barcelona a stylish, 21st-century metropolis, with a unique edge that adds to its allure.

Facts + Figures

- **Population: 1,673,075**
- **Area: City 99sq km (38sq miles)**
- **Highest point in Barcelona: Tibidabo (542m/1,777ft)**
- **9,533 cargo ships, 2,439 ferries and 706 cruise ships used the Port of Barcelona in 2006**

NO BULL

Barcelonins' self-view as a nation apart includes a widely held opposition to that quintessential Spanish passion, the bullfight. Animal rights supporters won the day in the 1970s when the last bull was killed in Las Arenas, the city's bullring. Today, it's being transformed into a shopping, office and leisure complex designed by Sir Richard Rogers.

CLIMBING THE CASTLE

Seize the chance to catch the *castellers*, clubs of locals who build human castles up to 10 levels high on high days and holidays. Participants climb upon each others shoulders to form 15m (50ft) constructions, traditionally topped by a child of 5 or 6, the *anxaneta*. The real heroes are the stalwarts taking the strain at the bottom level.

BEAUTIFUL BARÇA

FC Barcelona plays at Nou Camp, Europe's biggest stadium, with a 98,000 capacity. Their fan club, whose members are known as *los culés*, numbers more than 125,000 members, distinguished by their red-and-blue scarves, *de rigueur* on match days. Their arch enemy is Real Madrid; cheers issue from every bar in the city when Barça sees them off.

A Short Stay in Barcelona

DAY 1

Morning Start your day early in the **Barri Gòtic** (▷ 49), taking in the **Catedral** (▷ 42), the **Plaça de Sant Jaume** (▷ 48) and the **Plaça del Rei** (▷ 46), where, if your imagination's fired by the sense of history here, you can learn more at the **Museu d'Història de la Ciutat** (▷ 46). By 11.30, things are livening up on the **Ramblas** (▷ 44), so stroll up and down, perhaps pausing for a coffee, to soak up the atmosphere of Barcelona's most iconic thoroughfare. Take in the flower-sellers and street entertainers and then, if you've got the energy, walk along the waterfront beside the **Port Vell** (▷ 68) before heading up via Laietana and turning right into the **Ribera** (▷ 73), one of Barcelona's oldest but coolest areas.

Lunch Enjoy a quintessentially Spanish lunch of freshly prepared *tapas* at **Taller de Tapas** (▷ 58) on carrer Argentaria.

Afternoon Head down the street for the Plaça Santa Maria and spend a quiet moment in the beautiful Gothic church of **Santa Maria del Mar** (▷ 70) before heading up carrer Montcada, one of the old city's loveliest streets, to visit the **Museu Picasso** (▷ 63), housed in a series of stunning late medieval merchants' houses.

Dinner Cross the via Laietana and head through carrer Jaume I and down carrer Ferran for a drink at an outdoor table in the elegant **Plaça Reial** (▷ 51) before sampling a real Catalan dinner at **Can Culleretes** (▷ 57) just up the street, where classic local cooking has been served since 1786.

Evening Walk north through the old city, or take a taxi, to enjoy a performance in the stunning *modernista* surroundings of the **Palau de la Música Catalana** (▷ 64).

Morning Take the blue-route Bus Turístic in the **Plaça de Catalunya** (▷ 51) and sit back for the half-hour or so ride to **Montjuïc** (▷ 30). Alight at the **Museu Nacional d'Art de Catalunya** (▷ 28), pausing on the terrace to take in the city views. Spend a couple of hours in the museum, perhaps concentrating on the superb Romanesque fresco collection. If more culture appeals, hop back on the bus and take in either the **Fundació Joan Miró** (▷ 26), on the other side of Montjuïc or the **Museu Marítim** (▷ 24), at the foot of the Ramblas, before heading along the waterfront to **Barceloneta** (▷ 62).

Lunch Have lunch with the locals at the **Can Solé** (▷ 77), a great seafood restaurant with a fabulous selection of paellas, fresh fish, lobsters and prawns, before returning to Plaça de Catalunya.

Afternoon Change to a red-route bus, which will take you up the passeig de Gràcia, where you can get off to visit the **Manzana de la Discòrdia** (▷ 86), a block containing a trio of compelling *modernista* houses, and then walk north to visit Gaudí's most famous civil building the **Casa Milà** (▷ 84). From here, head east to his most famous creation, the **Sagrada Familia** (▷ 90). By 6, the streets around the passeig de Gràcia will be bustling, and it's a good time for some serious retail therapy.

Dinner Round off your homage to *modernisme* with a late-ish dinner at **Casa Calvet** (▷ 97), an innovative restaurant housed in a Gaudí-designed building.

Evening You could end the day with a couple of hours' partying at **Luz de Gas** (▷ 96), with its variety of live acts, or simply wind down over a late-night drink at a bar.

Top 25

►►►

Barceloneta ▷ 62
Densely built 18th-century fishermen's quarter famous for its village ambience.

Shopping in the Barri Gòtic ▷ 49 Discover the specialist shops, galleries, boutiques and chain stores in this maze of streets in the oldest part of the city.

Santa Maria del Mar ▷ 70–71 Barcelona's most beautiful Gothic church, Our Lady of the Sea dominates the Born area.

Sagrada Família ▷ 90–91 Gaudí's great visionary project, and Barcelona's most famous site, is still a long way from completion.

Las Ramblas ▷ 44–45 Strolling along Barcelona's most famous street is a must-do experience.

Port Vell ▷ 68–69 Seafront development whose shopping and entertainment draws the crowds.

Port Olímpic and the Beaches ▷ 67 Marinas, promenades and sandy beaches attract the crowds.

Casa Milà ▷ 84–85 Gaudí's controversial apartment block is one of the icons of the city.

Catedral ▷ 42–43 Barcelona's great cathedral is a splendid example of Catalan Gothic architecture.

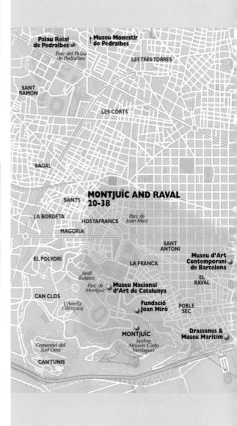

Plaça de Sant Jaume ▷ 48 This impressive square is the historical and political heart of the city.

Plaça del Rei ▷ 46–47 Beautiful medieval square with some of the city's most historic buildings.

Park Güell ▷ 88–89 Gaudí's amazing hilltop park is considered one of the city's treasures.

These pages are a quick guide to the Top 25, which are described in more detail later. Here they are listed alphabetically, and the tinted background shows the area they are in.

EL CARMEL
LA FONT D'EN FARGUES
Park Güell
LA SALUT
L'EIXAMPLE 79–98
Parc del Guinardó
EL GUINARDÓ
GRÀCIA
EL CAMP DE L'ARPA
Casa Milà (La Pedrera)
L'EIXAMPLE
SAGRADA FAMÍLIA
Sagrada Família
Manzana de la Discòrdia
LAS RAMBLAS AND THE BARRI GÒTIC 39–58
EL FORT PIUS
LAS RAMBLAS
PORT VELL AND LA RIBERA 59–78
BARRI GÒTIC
Palau de la Música Catalana
Plaça del Rei
CASC ANTIC
POBLE NOU
Catedral
Museu Picasso
Plaça de Sant Jaume
RIBERA Parc de la Ciutadella
Santa Maria del Mar
Parc Zoològic
Palau de Mar
Parc de la Barceloneta
Parc del Port Olímpic
Parc de Poblenou
Port Vell
BARCELONETA
Port Olímpic

◀ ◀ ◀

Shopping

Rich and stylish, as attractive to locals and Spaniards from outside Catalonia as it is to foreigners, the city rates as Spain's number-one shopping destination after Madrid. The contrast between tiny, old-world specialist shops and the glittering bastions of 21st-century retail therapy is striking; shops vary from the ultra-modern to relics from the past.

Leather Goods and Souvenirs

Branches of some of Spain and Europe's best-known fashion sources are here, as well as haunts for urban trendies, which stock classy and coquettish clothes with a twist. Added to that there's a wealth of serious, well-priced leather goods—shoes of every style and shade, bags of all descriptions, and deliciously supple belts, gloves and purses. As for souvenirs of this city of Gaudí, look for useful items with a *modernisme* theme—calendars and art books, vibrant ceramics and porcelain. The textiles are inspired; you can pick up gorgeous throws and fabrics in seductive shades and textures both from specialist shops and workshops.

Designer Bargains

For those who find the temptation of a designer bargain irresistible, a visit to La Roca Company Stores (www.larocavillage.com) will probably be essential. A 30-minute drive from Barcelona are exciting top brands at discounted prices, all in a pretty, 19th-century Catalan village.

WHERE TO SHOP

Plaça Catalunya is the place for department store shopping at El Corte Ingles and El Triangle shopping mall, while the Passeig de Gràcia has the big-name stores. Quirky shops are scattered throughout the Raval, Gràcia and El Born in the Ribera, Barcelona's hippest 'hood. The Barri Gòtic is great for crafts and antiques; there is a weekend art and bric-a-brac market held outside the port at the southern tip of Las Ramblas and in front of the Cathedral on Thursday. The best flea market is Els Encants at Plaça de la Glories.

Barcelona offers a wealth of fashionable shops, from main street stores to exclusive boutiques

Edible Gifts
Edible gifts are always popular; the Spanish specialty, *turrón* (nougat), almonds and olives spring to mind. Head for the Boqueria market and you'll find items such as strings of dried peppers, aromatic honey, golden threads of saffron, sheets of dried cod, superb hams and wonderful cheeses. Spanish nuts and dried fruits are superb, and exciting chocolate boutiques are popping up everywhere.

Crafts and Ceramics
Many craft objects can be picked up for a couple of euros. Basic beige and yellow ceramics from Catalonia's Costa Brava are inexpensive and plentiful. Reproduction *modernista* tiles are a stunning asset to bathrooms and kitchens. The *alpargatara*, the Catalan espadrille (rope sandal), usually has two-tone ribbons that wrap around the ankle, making stylish summer shoes. Most of these items can be picked up in souvenir shops, but they are likely to be mass-produced, so try and seek them out in specialty stores.

Specialist Shops
The old city is the home of Barcelona's best specialist shops. Trawling through the narrow streets of the Barri Gòtic and Raval you'll come across tiny shops devoted to wonderfully esoteric merchandise. There's even a shop devoted entirely to feathers. If you fancy a silk shawl, *mantilla* or intricate fan you'll find it here, as well as deliciously scented candles, flamenco dresses, traditionally made perfumes, soaps and cosmetics.

There are plenty of gift-buying opportunities in Barcelona—specialist food and craft shops abound

THE RAVAL
Along the narrow streets of the Raval, west of the Ramblas, you will find some of Barcelona's most interesting and one-of-a-kind shops. This is the place to hunt down red-hot design, second-hand fashion, clubwear and dance accessories. Look especially on and around carrer Riera Baixa, which is home to a Saturday alternative street market, and the Rambla del Raval, which has a market on weekends.

Shopping by Theme

Whether you're looking for a department store, a quirky boutique or something inbetween, you'll find it all in Barcelona. On this page shops are listed by theme. For a more detailed write-up, see the individual listings in Barcelona by Area.

ARTS, CRAFT AND DESIGN

Alamacen Marabi (▷ 74)
Alea Majoral Galéria de Joyas (▷ 74)
Art Escudellers (▷ 53)
D Baracelona (▷ 74)
Coses de Casa (▷ 53)
Cereria Subirá (▷ 53)
Dom (▷ 94)
Ganiveteria Roca (▷ 54)
Gotham (▷ 54)
Kitsch (▷ 74)
Sala Parés (▷ 54)
Vinçon (▷ 95)

BOOKS AND MUSIC

Altaïr (▷ 94)
BCN Books (▷ 94)
Castelló (▷ 36)

FASHION

Adolfo DomÍnguez (▷ 94)
Antonio Miro (▷ 95)
Armand Basi (▷ 94)
Le Boudoir (▷ 53)
Comité (▷ 36)
Como Agua de Mayo (▷ 74)
Custo Barcelona (▷ 36)
Desigual (▷ 94)
Jordi Lambanda (▷ 94)
Josep Font (▷ 95)
Lobby (▷ 75)
Mango (▷ 95)
Massimo Dutti (▷ 95)
On Land (▷ 75)

Menchén Tomás (▷ 75)
Sephora (▷ 95)
Snö Mito Nordico (▷ 95)

FOOD SHOPS AND MARKETS

La Bottifereria de Santa María (▷ 74)
Bubo (▷ 74)
Caelum (▷ 53)
Casa Gispert (▷ 74)
Colmado Quilez (▷ 94)
La Colmena (▷ 53)
Formatgeria La Seu (▷ 54)
Mercat de Santa Caterina (▷ 75)
Olive (▷ 75)
Papabubble (▷ 54)
Vila Viniteca (▷ 75)

GIFTS AND ANTIQUES

Arlequí Mascares (▷ 74)
Barri Gòtic Antiques Market (▷ 53)
Bulevard dels Antiquaris (▷ 94)
Caelum (▷ 53)
El Ingenio (▷ 54)
Els Encants Flea Market (▷ 95)
Joguines Monforte (▷ 54)
Plaça Reial: Coin and Stamp Market (▷ 54)
Plaça de Sant Josep Oriol: Picture Market (▷ 54)

MALLS AND DEPARTMENT STORES

Bulevard Rosa (▷ 94)
El Corte Inglés (▷ 53)
L'Illa (▷ 95)
Maremagnum (▷ 75)
El Triangle (▷ 54)

SHOES AND ACCESSORIES

Alamacenes de Pilar (▷ 53)
Camper (▷ 94)
Glamoor (▷ 74)
La Manual Alpargatera (▷ 54)
Minu Madhu (▷ 75)
Tous (▷ 95)
Vialis (▷ 36)

Barcelona by Night

The Rambla (▷ 44–45), the perfect place to stroll, pause and relax, acts like a magnet for an evening *paseo*. Amble up and down its length a couple of times, then grab a table at one of the many cafés and watch the world go by. Alternatively, start at the somewhat seedily elegant Plaça Reial (▷ 51) nearby. Other pleasant areas to stroll include the waterfront and Port Vell (▷ 68–69) and the Eixample for its wide boulevards, most notably the Passeig de Gràcia and Rambla Catalunya. The streets of the Barri Gòtic are also atmospheric.

Music, Theatre, Dance and Film
Barcelona has a good schedule of cultural evening events. The choice is wide, with everything from opera, orchestral concerts, plays and original language films to jazz, flamenco and Latin American music. You can get information in the weekly entertainment guide *Guia del Ocio* and from the Virreina Cultural Information Centre on the Rambla (☎ 93 316 10 00), or call the 010 information line, where an English-speaking operator will help.

Clubbing the Night Away
Barcelona is a clubber's paradise, with frequent visits from internationally famous DJs, plenty of homegrown talent and a constantly evolving scene. Clubs and bars open and close frequently so pick up flyers and check the listings in *Barcelona Metropolitan* and *Guia del Ocio*.

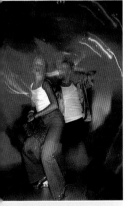

Barcelona's diverse nightlife includes some of Europe's top venues, clubs and bars

---

PICK OF THE PANORAMAS
From the slopes of Tibidabo, the huge peak towering behind the city, there are views over the whole city to the sea, and the area is well endowed with bars and cafés. The mountain's name comes from the Latin *tibi dabo*–'to thee I give', the words used by the Devil when tempting Christ. Another great view can be had from Montjüic, where there are green spaces to enjoy on summer evenings. Take the *teleféric* up to the castle for a bird's-eye view over the hill and the port below.

Eating Out

Eating out in this city is a pleasure, with the emphasis firmly on seasonal and fresh produce, and a huge range of restaurants, snack bars, *tapas* bars, cafés and *granjas* feeding residents and visitors day and night.

Breakfast
In hotels, breakfast may be included in the price, otherwise head for a bar or café. Most Catalans go for a *café con leche* (milky coffee) and croissant for breakfast, but *flautas* (french bread sticks) filled with cheese and charcuterie are nearly always available. For a cooked breakfast, *platos combinados* are combinations of fried eggs with bacon, sausages and tomatoes.

Lunch
Lunch, the main meal (*almuerzo*, or *dinar* in Catalan) is served between 2 and 4, and is traditionally the most important meal of the day. Most restaurants serve a *menú del dia*, a fixed-price menu, which is often excellent value.

Dinner
Dinner, *cena* (*sopar* in Catalan) starts after 9 and continues until midnight, though visitor-orientated restaurants open as early as 8. It's generally a lighter meal than lunch.

Snacks and *Tapas*
Granjas are great for a cake or pastry with coffee, milk shakes (*batidos*) and thick hot chocolate topped with whipped cream (*suizos*). *Tapas* range from a few olives or almonds to tortilla, chunks of meat and fish, cured ham and salads.

RESERVATIONS
Booking is advised in mid- to upper-price restaurants, particularly for groups of four or more and on the weekends. For less formal places, such as *tapas* bars, you can walk in and secure a table, even if you have to wait at the bar for a space to become available. However, if there is an establishment you really want to visit, check out whether booking is necessary.

There is a huge variety of restaurants and cafés at which to enjoy Barcelona's wonderful local produce

ESSENTIAL BARCELONA   EATING OUT

Restaurants by Cuisine

There are restaurants to suit all tastes and budgets in Barcelona. On this page they are listed by cuisine. For a more detailed description of each restaurant, see Barcelona by Area.

BODEGAS, CAFÉS AND TAPAS BARS

Bar del Pí (▷ 57)
Bodega de Palma (▷ 57)
Bodega Sepúlveda (▷ 38)
La Bombeta (▷ 77)
Cacao Sampaka (▷ 97)
Cata 1.81 (▷ 97)
Café de l'Opera (▷ 57)
Cerveceria Catalana (▷ 97)
Mam i Teca (▷ 38)
Quimat & Quimet (▷ 38)
Taller de Tapas (▷ 58)
Vinateria del Call (▷ 58)

CATALAN

Agut (▷ 57)
Alkimia (▷ 97)
Can Culleretes (▷ 57)
Casa Calvet (▷ 97)
Comerç 24 (▷ 78)
Jaume de Provença (▷ 98)
Jean Luc Figueras (▷ 98)
L'Olivé (▷ 98)
Pitarra (▷ 58)
Els Quatre Gats (▷ 58)
Set Portes (▷ 78)

INTERNATIONAL

Bestial (▷ 77)
Café de l'Academia (▷ 57)
Chido One (▷ 97)
Cinc Sentits (▷ 98)
Kynoto (▷ 57)
Little Italy (▷ 78)
La Locanda (▷ 58)
Noti (▷ 98)
Pla (▷ 58)
Le Relais de Venise (▷ 98)
Silenus (▷ 38)

MEDITERRANEAN

Ánima (▷ 38)
El Magatzem del Port (▷ 78)
Pla des Angels (▷ 38)
Sal Café (▷ 78)
Tapioles 53 (▷ 38)
Taxidermista (▷ 58)

NOUVELLE CUISINE

Moo (▷ 98)

REGIONAL SPANISH

Agua (▷ 77)
El Asador de Burgos (▷ 97)
Botafumerio (▷ 97)
Can Ramonet (▷ 77)
Centre Cultural Euskal Etxea (▷ 77)
Las Fernandez (▷ 38)
Mesón David (▷ 38)

SEAFOOD

El Cangrejo Loco (▷ 77)
Can Solé (▷ 77)
Cava Mar (▷ 77)
La Paradeta (▷ 78)
El Passadis d'en Pep (▷ 78)

VEGETARIAN

Habaluc (▷ 98)
Juicy Jones (▷ 57)

A friendly welcome at a Barcelonan restaurant

If You Like...

However you'd like to spend your time in Barcelona, these top suggestions should help you tailor your ideal visit. Each sight or listing has a fuller write-up in Barcelona by Area.

A LAZY MORNING

Stroll down Las Ramblas (▷ 44–45) and take in the flower stalls and street entertainment.
Relax over a drink in the faded grandeur of the Plaça Reial (▷ 51).
Enjoy the cool greenery, lake and fountains in the Parc de la Ciutadella (▷ 66).

WATERSIDE LIFE

Head for the Port Vell (▷ 68–69) for shops, walkways and cafés in a glorious seafront setting.
Take a harbour trip in the *golondrinas* (▷ 68).
Visit the Aquàrium to discover what's under the sea (▷ 69).

Mercat de la Boqueria (above), a shop in the Ribera (below) and Parc de la Ciutadella (bottom)

A TOUCH OF RETAIL THERAPY

Buy a ticket for the Tombbus, a luxury coach that covers the city's main shopping areas.
Trawl the narrow streets of the Barri Gòtic (▷ 49), the Raval (▷ 35) and the Ribera (▷ 73) for some of the city's most individualistic stores.
Hit the Boqueria market on the Ramblas (▷ 53) for a spread of food stalls that's among the best in the Med.

VISITING THE CULTURE TRAIL

Trace the artistic development of one of the world's foremost 20th-century creators at the Museu Picasso (▷ 63).
Explore the Barri Gòtic (▷ 52) with its ancient cathedral and museums.
Let the vibrant pictures and sculptures in the Fundació Joan Miró fill you in on the spirit of Barcelona (▷ 26–27).

A cablecar view of the port (below) and the Parc de la Ciutadella (below middle)

MOVING WITH STYLE

For a taste of the past, take a horse-drawn carriage round the Ramblas and waterfront.

Soar high above the port area by the cablecar that runs from Barceloneta to Montjuïc.

Hire a bike from any one of the dozens of outlets or at the tourist offices.

SIGHTS FOR SORE EYES

Take the elevator to the cathedral roof for a bird's-eye view of the Barri Gòtic (▷ 42–43).

See all Barcelona spread at your feet from the top of the Torre de Collserola on Tibidabo (▷ 106).

For ever-changing city views, stroll through the landscaped greenery of Montjuïc (▷ 30–31).

Peer down at the port area from the top of the Monument a Colom at the bottom of the Ramblas (▷ 68).

ROMANTIC RESTAURANTS

A classic Catalan salad (above) and the Bestial restaurant by night (below)

Enjoy the best of Catalan traditional cuisine in the 18th-century surroundings of Can Culleretes (▷ 57), where a series of rambling rooms is decorated with oil paintings and signed photos.

Relax under a parasol on the decking of Bestial and watch the sea while you eat Italian-style (▷ 77).

Soak up the atmosphere while you enjoy old-fashioned service and surroundings par excellence at the Set Portes (▷ 78).

Spend an evening dining in a Gaudí building at the Casa Calvet (▷ 97).

MODERNISME

Gaudí mosaic in Parc Güell (below) and the beach at Barceloneta (below middle)

See it in all its variations by taking in the Manzana de la Discòrdia on passeig de Gràcia—three different houses by the biggest names in *modernista* architecture (▷ 86–87).

Relax in a sumptuous interior at the Palau de la Música Catalana (▷ 64), where *modernista* decorative arts and music come together.

Take in *modernisme's* most iconic emblem, Gaudí's Sagrada Familia (▷ 90–91).

FRESH AIR AND GREEN SPACES

Combine fresh air and green space with *modernista* buildings and mosaics in the Park Güell (▷ 88–89).

Take the kids to Montjuïc for grass, plants and trees in downtown Barcelona (▷ 30–31).

SOMETHING FOR NOTHING

Entertainment in the shape of street performers is free to everyone along the Ramblas (▷ 44–45).

Sunbathing and swimming on Barcelona's beaches is a great way to have a free day out (▷ 67).

Take in some free culture by admiring the plethora of street sculpture that adorns the city.

A street entertainer in the Ramblas (above)

ENTERTAINING YOUR KIDS

Kids can let off steam on bikes and skates or visit the Parc Zoològic in the Parc de la Ciutadella (▷ 66).

The Aquàrium and the IMAX cinema at the Port Vell are top of the list for many young visitors (▷ 68–69).

The Aquàrium at the Port Vell (right)

Barcelona by Area

The hill of Montjuïc combines its role as a recreational area and a cultural stronghold with style, drawing in thousands of visitors. It overlooks the Raval, which underwent a major clean-up in the 1990s.

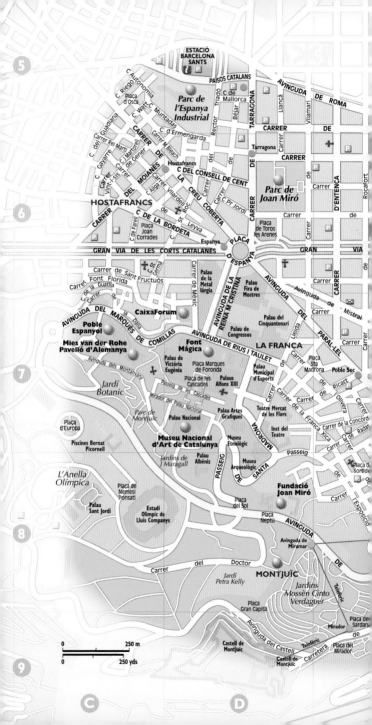

VALÈNCIA

D'ARAGÓ

del | VILADOMAT | Consell | de | Cent
Calàbria | la | Diputació
Rocafort | DE | LES | CORTS | CATALANES
| | Urgell
SANT | de | Comte | Sepúlveda
ANTONI | de | | Floridablanca
de | | Tamarit
Carrer | de | Manso
Carrer | Carrer | Parlament

D'URGELL
CARRER DE CASANOVA
DE MUNTANER
CARRER D'ARIBAU

Universitat
Central

PLAÇA DE LA
UNIVERSITAT

Plaça
Goya

Plaça
de
Castella

Carrer
Valldoncella
C de Tigre
Carrer de la
Paloma

Centre de Cultura
Contemporania
de Barcelona

**Museu d'Art
Contemporani**
Foment de les
Arts Decoratives

Carrer
del Peu de la Creu

CARRER | DEL | CARME

EL
RAVAL

CARRER | DE | L'HOSPITAL

**Antic
Hospital
Santa Creu**

C del Marquès
de Campo Sagrado

Santa
Madrona

Carrer
Aldana

C del Marquès
de Tapioles

Carrer Salva

Carrer del Roser

POBLE
SEC

Carrer | de | la | Rambla

C de Lafont

de | Cabanes

Carrer

Paral·lel

AVINGUDA

Margarit

Poeta

Cabanyes

Carrer

Nou

Passeig

MIRAMAR

de Miramar

Plaça
Carles
Ibàñez

Montjuïc

Jardins de
Miramar

Jardins del
Josep Costa
i Llobera

C l'Aurora

Carrer de les Carretes

Rambla del Raval

Rafael

Sant

Pau

C del Marquès de
Barbera

Carrer Nou de la Rambla

**Sant Pau
del Camp**

Carrer

de

Vila

Carrer Palaudàries

Carrer Puig Xi

Plaça de
l'Armada

PASSEIG | DE | JOSEP

RONDA | LITORAL

Montjuïc

Carrer Robador

Carrer Junta de Com

de l'Arc del Teatre

C Guàrdia

C Monts

**Drassanes &
Museu Marítim**

PLAÇA DE
DRASSANES | CARNER

ESTACIÓ
MARÍTIMA

E | F | G

Drassanes and Museu Marítim

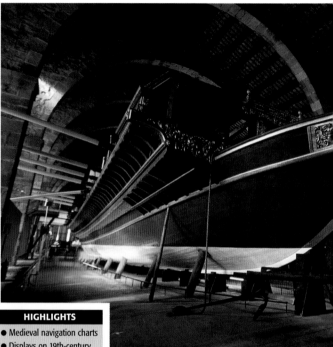

HIGHLIGHTS

- Medieval navigation charts
- Displays on 19th-century submarine *Ictíneo*
- Figurehead collection
- Fishing caravel of 1907

Great Adventure of the Sea

- Catalan Seapower in the 19th century
- Steamships and Emigration
- The Submarine World

TIPS

- Pick up the audio tour, the Great Sea Adventure, to get the best out of your visit.
- Come in the afternoon to avoid the school parties.

Cut off from today's port by cobbled docksides, the Gothic buildings of the Royal Shipyards are an evocative reminder of Barcelona's long-standing affair with the sea, as well as a unique monument to the Middle Ages.

Cathedral of the sea By the 13th century, Catalan sea power extended over much of the western Mediterranean. Ships were built in the covered Royal Shipyards, or Drassanes, a series of parallel halls with roofs supported on high arches. The effect is of sheer grandeur—of a cathedral rather than a functional workspace.

Ships on show The Drassanes are now a fascinating museum, displaying paintings, charts, model ships and all kinds of maritime memorabilia

The **Galera Real** *is one of the finest boats on display in the museum (below left and right), and includes some superbly detailed artwork (bottom)*

as well as a number of boats. These are all upstaged by the *Galera Real*, a full-size reproduction of the galley from which Don Juan d'Austria oversaw the defeat of the Turkish navy at the Battle of Lepanto in 1571. Built to commemorate the 400th anniversary of the battle, this elegant vessel is nearly 20m (65ft) long. The original was propelled to victory at high speed by chained galley slaves. You can see statues of some of them, along with the commander, who stands in the ornate stern, from a high catwalk, which also gives you a view of the building itself. Housed in a large exhibition hall, the *Galera Real* forms part of an exciting multimedia exhibit, where you can explore ships and warehouses and watch oarsmen bent over their galley oars. Through visual and acoustic effects, Catalonia's seafaring history is brought vividly to life.

THE BASICS

www.museummaritim-barcelona.org

✚ F8

✉ Avinguda de les Drassanes

☎ 93 342 99 20

🕐 Daily 10–8. Closed 1 Jan, 6 Jan, 24–25 Dec

🚇 Drassanes

🚌 14, 36, 38, 57, 59, 64, 91

♿ Few

💲 Expensive

Fundació Joan Miró

HIGHLIGHTS

● Painting, *The Morning Star*, dedicated to Miró's widow
● *Personage* (1931)
● Surrealist *Man and Woman in front of a pile of excrements* (1935)
● Barcelona Series (1939–44) Civil War graphics
● Anthropomorphic sculptures on roof terrace
● *Tapis de la Fundació* tapestry (1979)

TIP

● To avoid long walks or lengthy waits for local buses, use the Bus Turístic to access the Montjuïc museums.

Poised on the flank of Montjuïc is this white-walled temple to the art of Joan Miró, its calm interior spaces, patios and terraces are an ideal setting for the works of this most Catalan of all artists.

Miró and Barcelona Born in Barcelona in 1893, Joan Miró never lost his feeling for the city and the surrounding countryside, though he spent much of the 1920s and 1930s in Paris and Mallorca. His paintings and sculptures, with their intense primary colours and swelling, dancing and wriggling forms, are instantly recognizable, but he also gained renown for his expressive ceramics and graphic drawings inspired by political turmoil in Spain. Miró's distinctive influence is visible in graphic work all over Barcelona and locals as well as tourists flock to the Foundation, which is also a

Sculpture in the grounds at the Fundació Joan Miró (below left). Ten thousand of Miró's works are on display, including this vibrant woven tapestry (below right)

cultural hub dedicated to the promotion of contemporary art. It houses changing exhibitions, concerts, a library, shops and a café. Miró's works (11,000 in all, including 240 paintings) are complemented by those of numerous contemporaries including Balthus, Calder, Duchamp, Ernst, Léger, Matisse and Moore.

Mediterranean masterpiece The monumental yet intimate Foundation was built in 1974 by Miró's friend and collaborator, the architect Josep-Luis Sert, in a style that remains modern, yet traditionally Mediterranean in its use of forms such as domes, arches, and roof and terracotta floor tiles. It sits easily in the landscape, and its interpenetrating spaces incorporate old trees like the ancient olive in one of the courtyards. There are glorious views over the city, especially from the roof terrace.

THE BASICS

www.bcn.fjmiro.es

✚ D8

✉ Parc de Montjuïc

☎ 93 443 94 70

🕐 Jul–end Sep Tue–Sat 10–8 (Thu 10–9.30), Sun and hols 10–2.30; Oct–end Jun Tue–Sat 10–7 (Thu 10–9.30), Sun and hols 10–2.30. Closed 1 Jan, 24 Jun, 25 Dec

🍴 Café-restaurant

Ⓜ Espanya

🚌 61, 50

🚠 Montjuïc funicular from Paral.lel Metro

♿ Good

💰 Moderate

❓ Book and gift shop

27

Museu Nacional d'Art de Catalunya

TOP 25

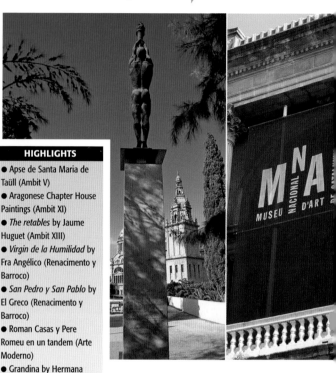

HIGHLIGHTS

● Apse de Santa Maria de Taüll (Ambit V)
● Aragonese Chapter House Paintings (Ambit XI)
● *The retables* by Jaume Huguet (Ambit XIII)
● *Virgin de la Humilidad* by Fra Angélico (Renacimento y Barroco)
● *San Pedro y San Pablo* by El Greco (Renacimento y Barroco)
● Roman Casas y Pere Romeu en un tandem (Arte Moderno)
● Grandina by Hermana Anglada Camarasa (Arte Moderno)
● *Furniture* by Gaudí from the Casa Batllo (Arte Moderno)

TIPS

● To avoid the uphill slog from the metro either take bus 55, the blue Bus Turístic or a taxi to reach the museum.
● Allow at least 2 hours for a visit.
● The museum has an excellent restaurant and a café.

The impressive Palau Nacional, which dominates the northern flank of Montjuïc, houses the National Museum of Catalan Art. Its mural paintings, sculpture, frescoes, woodcarvings and pictures combine to offer a staggeringly complete overview of a millennium of Catalan art.

Romanesque Riches The entire west wing of the ground floor concentrates on the museum's major treasure, the mural paintings rescued from isolated 10th-century churches high in the Pyrenees. This exceptionally rich heritage of Romanesque art was created as Christianity recolonized the mountain valleys during the 12th and 13th centuries. Powerful images of Christ in Majesty, the Virgin Mary and the saints promoted piety among a peasant population

The Palau Nacional provides a superb setting for the Museu Nacional d'Art de Catalunya and its extensive collection of Catalan art

recently released from the Moorish yoke. By the early 20th century, such art enjoyed little prestige and it was only through the heroic efforts of a dedicated band of art historians and archaeologists that so much was saved from decay and theft. There are 21 mural sections, loosely arranged in chronological order.

Medieval to Modernism Elsewhere in the museum the rooms are given over to a rich collection of Gothic art thanks to two important bequests. The Thyssen-Bornemisza and the Cambó collections include works from El Greco, Tintoretto, Titian and Rubens. Upstairs the MNAC holds a dazzling collection of modernista painting, furniture and decorative arts, much of it taken from the stately homes of the Eixample and including some fluid furniture from Gaudí.

THE BASICS

www.mnac.es
➕ D7
✉ Palau Nacional, Parc de Montjuïc
☎ 93 622 03 76
🕐 Tue–Sat 10–7, Sun and hols 10–2.30. Closed 1 Jan, 1 May, 25 Dec
🚇 Espanya
🚌 13, 37, 50, 55, 57, and all buses to Plaça Espanya
♿ Good
🎟 Moderate

Montjuïc

The Palau Sant Jordi stadium (below left) and the Plaça Sardana (below right)

THE BASICS

⊞ B8/9, C7/8/9, D7/8/9, E8/9
🍴 Restaurants and cafés
Ⓜ Espanya, Parallel (then funicular)
🚌 61, 50, 55 and PM (Parc Montjuïc) bus

HIGHLIGHTS

Buildings and structures
● Fundació Joan Miró (▷ 26–27)
● Magic fountains (Plaça Carlos Buigas)
● El Museu Militar for its fabulous views

Gardens
● Parc del Fossar de la Pedrera
● Mossen Costa I Llobera gardens
● Jardí Botànic
● Teatre Grec amphitheatre

Covering an area bigger than the Barri Gòtic, 'Jove's mountain' rises imposingly over the port. This is the city's finest park, a unique blend of exotic gardens and tourist attractions, including two of the city's finest museums.

Ancient beginnings Prehistoric people had settled here, high above the bay, long before the Romans built their shrine to Jove, and the hill's quarries were the source of stone from which half the old city was built. Montjuïc has also always been a place of burial, represented today in the Cimentiri del Sud-Oest on the hill's far flank. Crowning the summit is the castle, which now houses a military museum.

The 1929 Expo Montjuïc really came into its own in the 20th century. The Expo was preceded by a long period of preparation in which the slopes were terraced and planted to create the luxuriant landscape that exists today. Exhibition buildings were put up in a variety of styles ranging from the pompous Palau Nacional (▷ 28) to one of the key works of modern architecture, the Germany Pavilion by Mies van der Rohe (▷ 31). One of the Expo's main attractions was the Poble Espanyol (▷ 34) and the great City Stadium was second only to London's Wembley in size. When the Olympic Games came to Barcelona in 1992, Montjuïc became Mount Olympus; the Anella Olímpica (Olympic Ring) includes the splendidly restored stadium as well as the close-by flying-saucer-like Palau Sant Jordi.

More to See

CAIXAFORUM

www.fundacio.lacaixa.es

This stunning conversion of a *modernista* former textile factory was funded by La Caixa, Catalonia's largest savings bank. Its revamp gave it an entrance plaza, an auditorium, library and some of Barcelona's most impressive exhibition space. In addition to the permanent collection, major international temporary exhibitions are staged throughout the year; 2007's range included shows devoted to photographer Cindy Sherman and William Hogarth.

➕ D7 ✉ Casaramona, Avinguda del Marquès de Comillas 6–8 ☎ 93 476 86 00 ◉ Tue–Sun 10–8 (Sat until 10) ◉ Espanya 🖐 Free

FONT MÁGICA

Barcelona's 'magic fountain' is one of its most crowd-pleasing attractions. A relic of the 1929 international exhibition at the base of the stairs to the MNAC (▶ 28–29), the ornamental fountain looks pretty much like any other during the day. But come nightfall it comes to life with a spectacular light-and-music show—the water spurts 'dance' to the beats, while a rainbow of tinted lights add a Las Vegas-type neon glow to the water. Get there early to grab a seat at one of the outdoor cafés or limited public seating.

➕ D7 ✉ Plaça Buïgas 1 ◉ May–end Sep Thu–Sun 9pm–11.30pm; Oct–end Apr Fri and Sat 7am–9pm ◉ Espanya 🖐 Free

MIES VAN DER ROHE PAVELLÓ D'ALEMANYA

www.miesbcn.com

Germany's contribution to the Expo of 1929 was this supremely cool construction of steel, glass and marble that reinvented all the rules of architecture. It has become an icon of modern (as opposed to *modernista*) design. Yet amazingly, the building was demolished when the fair was over. It was rebuilt by devoted admirers in the mid-1980s and is now a compulsory stop for architecture students.

➕ C7 ✉ Pavelló Barcelona, Avinguda del Marquès de Comillas ☎ 93 423 40 16 ◉ Daily 10–8 ◉ Espanya 🖐 Moderate

The view inside the Olympic Stadium

Museu d'Art Contemporani

MONTJUÏC AND RAVAL   TOP 25

HIGHLIGHTS

Works in the collection (not
necessarily on show) by
● Miquel Barceló
● Jean-Michel Basquiat
● Joseph Beuys
● Antoni Clavé
● Xavier Grau
● Richard Long
● Robert Rauschenberg
● Antoni Tàpies

TIP

● The excellent bookshop
has a wide selection, including exhibition catalogues
from past shows, designer
classics and accessories.

**Could this be Barcelona's answer to
Paris's Centre Pompidou? A glittering
white home for late 20th-century art,
known as the MACBA, has given the
run-down inner city district of Raval an
ultra-modern shot in the arm.**

A modern museum For many years Barcelona
felt the lack of an adequate establishment devoted
to the contemporary visual arts. During the repres-
sive Franco years, its progressive artists enjoyed
little official encouragement. Now two major institutions are bringing it back into the mainstream.
By any reckoning, the Museum of Contemporary
Art is remarkable, though its long white walls and
huge size are strikingly at odds with the ram-
shackle façades of the surrounding buildings
across the wide modern *plaça* in an up and

The spectacular Richard Meier-designed Museu d'Art Contemporani de Barcelona was opened in 1995

coming part of town. The shining structure, designed by the American architect Richard Meier, opened in 1995. Its exhibition spaces lead to a great atrium and are reached by a spectacular series of ramps and glass-floored galleries, sometimes almost upstaging the works on display. Temporary exhibitions featuring local and international artists complement the museum's own extensive collection, which is exhibited in rotation.

Centre de Cultura Contemporània Housed adjacent in the striking old poor house buildings of the Casa de la Caritat, the Centre for Contemporary Culture promotes a range of activities focused on cultural and social themes. Each year sees a season of cultural and theatrical events exploring different aspects of contemporary art and style, from fashion and architecture to modern communications.

THE BASICS

www.macba.es
✚ F7
✉ Museum, Plaça dels Angels 1; Centre, Montalegre 5
☎ Museum: 93 412 08 10; Centre: 93 306 41 00
🕓 MACBA: 25 Sep–23 Jun Mon, Wed–Fri 12–8, Sat 10–8, Sun and hols 10–3; 24 Jun–24 Sep Mon, Wed–Fri 11–8 (Thu, Fri until midnight), Sun and hols 10–3. CCCB: Tue–Sun 11–8 (Thu until 10)
🚇 Catalunya, Universitat
🚌 9, 14, 24, 38, 41, 50, 54, 55, 58, 59, 64, 66, 91, and all routes to Plaça Catalunya
♿ Good 💶 Moderate

33

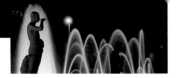

More to See

PARC DE L'ESPANYA INDUSTRIAL

The postmodern design of Europe's oddest municipal park flies in the face of all the rules in the landscape architect's book. Trees are almost outnumbered by the giant lighthouses on one side of the site; one plane tree grows out of a heap of rocks; and the Mediterranean sun beats down on the blinding white stairways. But children love the monster metal slide, styled to look like St. George and the Dragon, and there are always customers for the boats on the lake.

✚ D5 ✉ Rector Triado ◉ Open access ◎ Sants-Estació

PARC DE JOAN MIRÓ (PARC DE L'ESCORXADOR)

The sculptor's giant polychromatic *Woman and Bird* dominates this park with its orderly rows of palm trees. It is laid out on the site of an old slaughterhouse, l'Escorxador, where bulls were taken after fights.

✚ D6 ✉ Carrer de Tarragona ◉ Open access ◎ Tarragona, Espanya

POBLE ESPANYOL

www.poble-espanyol.com

Barcelona's 'Spanish Village' provides a whistle-stop tour of the country's architecture and urban scenery. Craft shops, cafés and restaurants and a new museum add to the appeal.

✚ C7 ✉ Avinguda Marquès de Comillas s/n ☎ 93 508 63 00 ◉ Sun 9–midnight, Mon 9–8, Fri–Sat 9–4am, Tue–Thu 9–2am (some shops/attractions close earlier) ◎ Espanya 🚌 13, 50, 61, and all routes to Plaça Espanya ♿ Moderate

SANT PAU DEL CAMP

This village church was in the middle of the countryside when it was built in the 12th century. It replaced an older building, probably dating from Visigothic times, which was wrecked by Moorish invaders; some material from this original building was used to build the columns. The façade's simple and severe sculptural decoration includes the symbols of the Evangelists and the Hand of God.

✚ F8 ✉ Carrer de Sant Pau 101 ◉ Mon–Fri noon–1, 7.30–8.30 ◎ Paral.lel

Poble Espanyol (above)

Sculpture at the Parc de Joan Miró (left)

A Walk Through El Raval

This walk gives a good chance to experience the atmosphere of this teeming and historic multi-ethnic working area.

DISTANCE: 2km (1.2 miles) **ALLOW:** 45–50 minutes

START

BOQUERIA MARKET ➕ G7 ▷ 50
🚇 Liceu

END

RONDA DE SANT ANTONI ➕ F6
🚇 Universitat

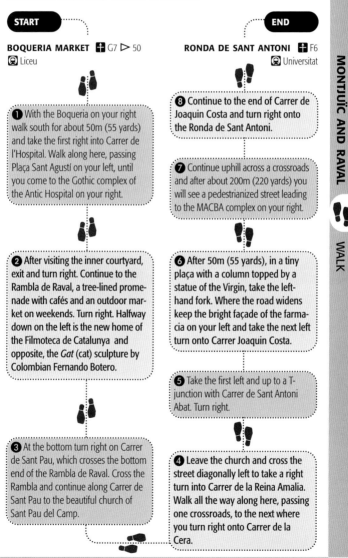

1 With the Boqueria on your right walk south for about 50m (55 yards) and take the first right into Carrer de l'Hospital. Walk along here, passing Plaça Sant Agustí on your left, until you come to the Gothic complex of the Antic Hospital on your right.

2 After visiting the inner courtyard, exit and turn right. Continue to the Rambla de Raval, a tree-lined promenade with cafés and an outdoor market on weekends. Turn right. Halfway down on the left is the new home of the Filmoteca de Catalunya and opposite, the *Gat* (cat) sculpture by Colombian Fernando Botero.

3 At the bottom turn right on Carrer de Sant Pau, which crosses the bottom end of the Rambla de Raval. Cross the Rambla and continue along Carrer de Sant Pau to the beautiful church of Sant Pau del Camp.

8 Continue to the end of Carrer de Joaquin Costa and turn right onto the Ronda de Sant Antoni.

7 Continue uphill across a crossroads and after about 200m (220 yards) you will see a pedestrianized street leading to the MACBA complex on your right.

6 After 50m (55 yards), in a tiny plaça with a column topped by a statue of the Virgin, take the left-hand fork. Where the road widens keep the bright façade of the farmacia on your left and take the next left turn onto Carrer Joaquin Costa.

5 Take the first left and up to a T-junction with Carrer de Sant Antoni Abat. Turn right.

4 Leave the church and cross the street diagonally left to take a right turn into Carrer de la Reina Amalia. Walk all the way along here, passing one crossroads, to the next where you turn right onto Carrer de la Cera.

MONTJUÏC AND RAVAL

WALK

Shopping

CASTELLÓ
A chain of music shops that stock varying specialities: Visit the Tallers 7 branch for pop, folk and world music and Tallers 3 for classical music.
G8 ✉ Tallers 3–9 ☎ 93 412 17 69 🚇 Liceu

COMITÉ
An eclectic selection of clothing from young local designers hang in this lovely shop, which has the decor of a pretty children's nursery. This theme often extends to the garments, with funny, animal print and appliqué, hand-covered buttons and pert bows.
G7 ✉ Carrer Notariat 8 ☎ 93 317 68 13 🚇 Liceu

CUSTO BARCELONA
The Custo brother's bright and funky T-shirts are now worn by trendsetters across the world from Toronto to Tokyo, but their hometown store has the best selection.
G7 ✉ Las Ramblas 109 ☎ 93 481 39 30 🚇 Liceu

ESCRIBA
Barcelona's finest *chocolateria* is housed in a lovely *modernista* building right on the Ramblas. Stop here for melt-in-the-mouth chocolates, cakes and to admire the extravagant chocolate creations.
G8 ✉ La Rambla 83 ☎ 93 301 60 27 🚇 Liceu

RIERA BAIXA SECOND-HAND MARKET
A pretty, pedestrianized street filled with retro boutiques, flea-market stores, costume houses and knick-knack emporiums. Visit on Saturday afternoon when the stores spill on to the pavement and vintage bargains abound.
G8 ✉ Carrer Riera Baixa 🚇 Sant Antoni

VIALIS
Beautiful handmade shoes from Mallorca combine artisan methods with hip design, and have quickly become the footwear of choice for trendy Barceloneses.
G7 ✉ Carrer Elisabets 20 ☎ 93 342 60 71 🚇 Liceu

Entertainment and Nightlife

BAR ALMIRALL
This atmospheric *fin de siècle* bar is famous for *absenta*, the supposedly hallucinogenic liquor preferred by 19th-century bohemians, though most locals settle into the cracked leather sofas with a glass of good whiskey.
G7 ✉ Carrer Joaquim Costa 33 ☎ No phone 🚇 Universitat

BAR LOBO
Trendy, two-floor tapas bar. Its outdoor terrace is a great spot for a drink, day or night. Thursday to Saturday select chill-out sessions in the upstairs lounge.
G7 ✉ Carrer Pintor Fortuny 3 ☎ 93 481 53 46 🚇 Liceu

CLUB APOLO
Old music hall that hosts live pop-rock nightly and dance clubs Thursday to Sunday.
G7/8 ✉ Carrer Nou de la Rambla 113 ☎ 93 441 40 01 🚇 Paral.lel

CLUB FELLINI
Rambla nighthawks and insomniacs love this place, as do packs of partying tourists. Its slightly grungy decor adds to the appeal, as does the 1980s-electro music, so you can pretty much bet on a packed house.
G8 ✉ Las Ramblas 27 ☎ 93 272 49 80 🚇 Drassanes

LONDON BAR
Here since 1910, this former bohemian establishment, later taken up by local hippies, now draws a cosmopolitan mix of locals and young foreign residents.

🔲 G8 ☒ Carrer Nou de la Rambla 34 ☎ 93 318 52 61 🚇 Paral.lel, Liceu

MERCAT DE LES FLORS
The splendid halls of the old flower market at the foot of Montjuïc are the main venue for the annual Grec Festival. During the rest of the year, there is a rich variety of dramatic, dance and concert events.
🔲 D7 ☒ Carrer de Lleida 59 ☎ 93 426 18 75 🚇 Espanya

MOOG
Techno goes full blast at one of the city's most popular clubs. Guest DJs from the international circuit. Chill-out room.
🔲 F/G8 ☒ Carrer de l'Arc del Teatre 3 ☎ 93 301 72 82 🕐 Daily 🚇 Drassanes

NEGRONI
This small, cleverly lit cocktail bar won a design award for its cutting-edge interior and would hold it's own on the streets of New York. Locals pack it on the weekends, vying for great cocktails at good prices.
🔲 G7 ☒ Carrer Joaquim Costa 4 ☎ 661 361 067 🚇 Liceu

PALAU SANT JORDI
This masterpiece of modern architecture—a stadium in the Olympic Games turned music barn—hosts many of the big-name bands that come to Barcelona.
🔲 C8 ☒ Passeig Olímpic s/n ☎ 93 426 20 89 🚇 Espanya

THE QUIET MAN
One of the city's best Irish bars has live Celtic music Thursday to Saturday.
🔲 G8 ☒ Marqués de Berbera 11 ☎ 93 412 12 19 🚇 Liceu

SPACE
The local version of the famous Ibizan club is a lot smaller, and in a nondescript office block area as opposed to the beach. A youngish, designer-clad crowd dance through to its 6am closure.
🔲 D6 ☒ Carrer Tarragona 141-147 ☎ 93 426 84 44 Tarragona

TABLAO DE CARMEN
This full-blooded flamenco show in touristy Poble Espanyol is none the worse for the setting—locals come here, too.

You can dine while watching the show, which is staged twice nightly.
🔲 C7 ☒ Poble Espanyol ☎ 93 325 68 95 🚇 Espanya 🚌 13, 61

LA TERRRAZZA
This huge, open-air, 'Ibiza-style' club, inside the Poble Espanyol, functions in summer as a place to dance the night away to some of the city's best dance music.
🔲 C/D7 ☒ Avinguda del Marqués de Comillas ☎ 93 272 49 80 🕐 May–Oct Thu–Sun from midnight 🚇 Espanya

TINTA ROJA
This lovely bar has a bohemian decor: ageing velvet armchairs, lead-light lamps and dark lace curtains give it the air of an old bordello. Known for its live tango music, but also hosts circus acts and drama groups.
🔲 E7 ☒ Carrer Creu dels Molers 17 ☎ 93 443 32 43 🚇 Poble Sec

MONTJUÏC AND RAVAL

ENTERTAINMENT AND NIGHTLIFE

Restaurants

ÁNIMA (€€)

This trendy place near the MACBA trumps other eateries in the vicinity by matching the quality of its food to the decor. A preferred place for lunch with local creative types who get there early for the outdoor terrace.
✚ G7 ✉ Carrer de Àngels 6 ☎ 93 342 49 12 🕐 Closed Sun 🚇 Liceu

BODEGA SEPÚLVEDA (€)

The excellent value *menú del día* usually includes a good seafood dish. Or try the varied *tapas*.
✚ F6 ✉ Carrer de Sepúlveda 173bis ☎ 93 454 70 94 🕐 Closed Sun 🚇 Urgell

LAS FERNANDEZ (€€)

For a taste of something other than Catalan food, head for this outpost of cooking from Leon, where three sisters offer meaty specialties such as dried venison, sausages and hams, as well as light Mediterranean dishes. Bright and cheerful.
✚ F7/8 ✉ Carrer de les Carretes 11 ☎ 93 443 20 43 🕐 Closed Mon and lunch 🚇 Paral·lel

MAM I TECA (€€)

Tiny hole-in-the-wall with few tables and a small bar. Local foodies love the regional *tapas* that changes most days. Top notch ingredients.
✚ F7 ✉ Carrer de Luna 4 ☎ 93 441 33 35 🕐 Closed Tue 🚇 Sant Antoni

MESÓN DAVID (€)

This wonderfully lively and friendly place offers some of the cheapest food in Barcelona. Standards are high and the accent is on Galician cuisine, with *caldo gallego* (cabbage broth) and succulent *lechazo* (roast pork) well to the fore. Sample the almond *tarta de Santiago* for pudding.
✚ F7/8 ✉ Carrer de les Carretes 63 ☎ 93 441 59 34 🕐 Closed Wed and Aug 🚇 Paral·lel

PLA DELS ANGELS (€)

A great place for lunch after a morning at MACBA, this well-designed, rainbow-bright

café-restaurant offers an excellent, good value *menú del día*, imaginative salads, good pasta and meat dishes and some of the richest chocolate experiences in town.
✚ F7 ✉ Carrer de Ferlandina 23 ☎ 93 329 40 47 🕐 Daily 🚇 Catalunya

QUIMET & QUIMET (€)

More a *bodega* than a bar, this incredibly popular joint has a great selection of wine behind the bar and and a fantastic selection of *tapas*.
✚ E8 ✉ Poeta Cabanyes 25 ☎ 93 442 31 42 🕐 Closed Sun, Sat dinner and Aug 🚇 Paral·lel

SILENUS (€€)

Relaxed spot serving modern Mediterranean with the accent on quirky interpretations of Catalan and Spanish dishes.
✚ G7 ✉ Angels 8 ☎ 93 302 26 80 🕐 Closed Sun 🚇 Liceu

TAPIOLES 53 (€€)

This intimate gastro club offers lovingly prepared, though light in portions, three-course meals using local ingredients. The focus is on Mediterranean cooking, but desserts, prepared by an American pastry chef, are rich and creamy cakes and pies. Reservations essential.
✚ E8 ✉ Carrer Tapioles 53 ☎ 93 329 22 38 🕐 Closed lunch and Sun, Mon 🚇 Poble Sec

Las Ramblas is Barcelona's magnet, a historic, tree-lined promenade that stretches south from the Plaça de Catalunya to the sea. To its east lies the Barri Gòtic, the ancient city heart.

Las Ramblas and Barri Gòtic

6

Universitat
Central

PLAÇA DE LA
UNIVERSITAT

Universitat

RONDA

CARRER DE BALMES

UNIVERSITAT

C DE

Carrer

PELAI

dels

Catalunya

Tallers

Catalunya

7

Casa Municipal
de Misericòrdia

C Elisabets

RAMBLA

C Sant

C Canuda

C Pintor Fortuny

CARRER DEL CARME

Palau de la
Virreina

La Boqueria

Església
de Betlem

Plaça
Vila d
Madri

i

BARR
GÒTIC

Plaça
de Pí

CARRER DE L'HOSPITAL

Santa
Maria de Pí

Liceu

C Boqueria

Carrer de Sant Pau

Gran Teatre
del Liceu

C de Ferran

Carrer Nou de la Rambla

Palau
Güell

RAMBLA

Plaça
Reial

C Codols

C Nou de St Francesc

Carre

C de l'Arc del Teatre

LA

Museu
de Cera

C de

Drassanes

PLAÇA
DEL PORTAL
DE LA PAU

Carrer J A Clavé

PASSEIG

DE

8

9

0   200 m
0   200 yds

F   G

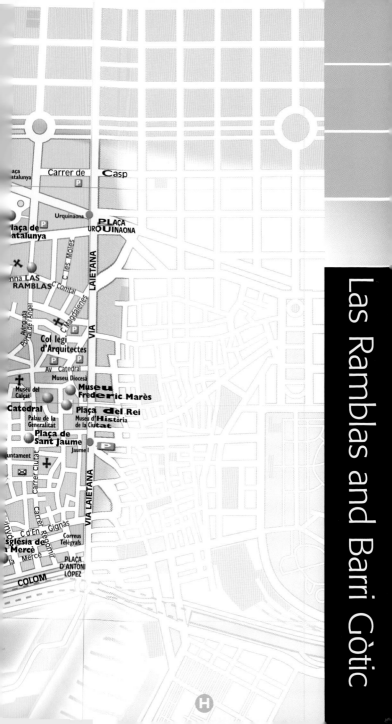

Carrer de Casp

Urquinaona

PLAÇA
UROUINAONA

aça
atalunya

laça de
atalunya

nna LAS
RAMBLAS

C. Contal

C. tes Moles

C Magdalenes

VIA LAIETANA

Avinguda
Portal de l'Àngel

Col·legi
d'Arquitectes

Av. Catedral

Museu Diocesà

Museu del
Calçat

Museu
Frederic Marès

Catedral

Plaça del Rei

Palau de la
Generalitat

Museu d'Història
de la Ciutat

Plaça de
Sant Jaume

Jaume I

untament

Carrer Ciutat

VIA LAIETANA

Carrer Ciutat

Carrer Regomir

C d'En Gignas

Correus
Telègrafs

glésia de
a Mercè

Mercè

PLAÇA
D'ANTONI
LÓPEZ

COLOM

H

Catedral

This 14th-century cathedral is one of the finest examples of the Catalan Gothic style. It is a noble successor to its Romanesque predecessor and an even older early Christian basilica.

City church Dedicated to an early Christian virgin and martyr, Eulàlia, the cathedral stands firmly in the middle of city life. Weekends see people gather to dance the elegant *sardana*, a stately Catalan folk dance that symbolizes unity. Inside, worshippers easily outnumber tourists. The cloister is a calm refuge from the city with its magnolias, tall palms, fountain and gaggle of geese.

Medley of styles The cathedral was begun at the end of the 13th century and was completed, except for the main façade, by the middle of the

The magnificent interior of the Catedral (far left). Votive candles at an altar (top middle). The imposing Gothic entrance (top right). Dancers performing the sardana (bottom centre). Statues adorning the cathedral exterior (bottom right)

15th. However, it was not until the mid-19th century that sufficient funds had been accumulated to construct the façade—fashionable but somewhat incongruous in its French-Gothic style. You could spend hours peering at the sometimes faded treasures in the 29 chapels. The most fascinating of these is the old chapter house to the right of the main entrance; beneath a roof rising 20m (65ft) into a star vault is the Christ of Lepanto, a life-size figure carried into the thick of the famous naval battle aboard the royal flagship (▷ 24–25).

The views The elevator on the opposite side to the cloister takes you to the roof from where magnificent panoramic views of the city and the cathedral's spires can be enjoyed from a platform placed over the central nave. The statue perched on top of the highest, central spire is of St. Helen.

THE BASICS

✚ G7
✉ Plaça de la Seu
☎ 93 310 71 95
🕐 Mon–Fri 8–12.45, 5–7.30, Sat 8–12.45, 5–6, Sun 5–6. VIP entry daily 1.30–4.30
🚇 Jaume I
🚌 17, 19, 40, 45
♿ Good
💵 VIP entry: moderate (includes elevator and choir, museum); museum, elevator and choir: inexpensive; everything else free

Las Ramblas

HIGHLIGHTS

Starting at Plaça de Catalunya
● Flower market
● Baroque Betlem Church
● 18th-century Palau Moja
● 18th-century Palau de la Virreina information area
● La Boqueria covered market (▷ 50)
● Gran Teatre del Liceu
● Mural by Miró on the pavement at the intersection of Carrer Boqueria
● Centre d'Art Santa Monica
● Museu de Cera (Wax Museum) (▷ 50)

TIPS

● Pickpocketing is rife on the Ramblas, so watch your bag and wallet.
● Bar and restaurant prices are high here and standards low—eat elsewhere.

Supreme among city strolling spaces, the Rambla stretches from Plaça de Catalunya to the waterfront. Venerable plane trees frame the broad central walkway, which teems with activity.

Pedestrian paradise Most Catalan towns have their Rambla, a promenade where people go to see and be seen. None, however, enjoys the worldwide fame of Barcelona's. Sooner rather than later, every visitor joins the crowds along this vibrant central space, where strollers rule and traffic is confined to either side. More than a mere thoroughfare, the Rambla is a place—somewhere to linger, to sit, to rendezvous, to watch street entertainers, to buy a paper, to simply breathe in the essence of the city. Until the 18th century, breathing deeply was highly inadvisable; the

The fountain in Rambla de Canaletes (left). Enjoying the Catalan sunshine (top middle). A flowerstand on Rambla de Sant Josep (bottom middle). One of the many specialist food shops on Las Ramblas (right)

Rambla owes its origin to an open sewer along the line of the city walls, which once stood here.

More than one Rambla The Rambla changes its name several times on its way down toward the Columbus Column, just over 1km (half a mile) from Plaça de Catalunya. First comes Rambla de Canaletes with its famous drinking fountain and newsstands, then Rambla dels Estudis, named for the university once sited here. The Rambla de Sant Josep is also known as Rambla de les Flors, after its profusion of flowerstands. The halfway point is marked by Miró's mosaic in the pavement and by Liceu subway station, named after the city's opera house. The Rambla dels Caputxins follows, with its cafés, then the Rambla de Santa Monica, which has retained its earthy charm despite attempts at modernization.

THE BASICS

G7/8
Catalunya, Liceu, Drassanes
14, 59, 91

Plaça del Rei

HIGHLIGHTS

Museu d'Història de la Ciutat

● Roman city streets, shops and workrooms
● Roman mosaics
● Saló del Tinell
● Chapel of St. Agatha: 15th-century altarpiece by Jaume Huguet

The Plaçe de Rei

● Steps to the palace
● Linger in an outdoor café

TIP

● The Museu d'Història is a great place to start your sightseeing by putting Barcelona's history in perspective.

There is no better way to experience the antiquity of the city than in the Roman settlement of Barcino, the underground world that extends beneath the medieval palace and the Plaça del Rei.

Remains of Roman Barcelona The middle of Roman Barcelona extends beneath Plaça de Sant Jaume and Plaça del Rei, while chunks of its walls protrude elsewhere. One of the best-preserved sections faces Plaça Ramon Berenguer el Gran, next to Plaça del Rei; above the Roman wall and towers are later layers of building, including the medieval Chapel of St. Agatha.

Museu d'Història de la Ciutat The City History Museum's exhibits trace Barcelona's evolution from Roman trading post to metropolis. The

The entrance to the Museu d'Història de la Ciutat (left). The museum was previously a medieval palace (right)

museum on Plaça del Rei occupies a medieval palace moved here in 1931 when the Via Laietana was driven through the Barri Gòtic. Remains of the old Roman town were revealed by excavations carried out during the rebuilding work. Mosaic floors and parts of surrounding walls are among the underground ruins accessible from the museum. Other relics from Barcelona's history include statues and an oil press.

Regal relics The visit continues above ground in the medieval palace. The highlight is the arched space of the 14th-century Saló del Tinell, the banquet hall where Columbus was received on his return from the New World. Also visit the Chapel of St. Agatha and admire the five-floor lookout tower Mirador del Rei Martí, named for King Martí, which is currently closed for renovations.

THE BASICS

➕ G8
☎ 93 315 11 11
🕐 Tue–Sat 10–2, 4–8 (Jul–end Sep 10–8); Sun and hols 10–3. Closed 1 Jan, 1 May, 24 Jun, 24 and 25 Dec
🚇 Jaume I
🚌 17, 19, 40, 45
♿ Poor
💶 Moderate. Ticket admits to museum, Roman remains, Saló del Tinell, chapel and tower.
❓ Souvenir and book-shop (entrance Carrer Llibreteria)
www.museuhistoria.bcn.es

Plaça de Sant Jaume

The Ajuntament (left and right) and a statue of St. George in the Generalitat (middle)

THE BASICS

Ajuntament
+ G8
☎ 93 402 70 00
🕑 Sun 10–2
🚇 Liceu, Jaume I
🚌 14, 17, 19, 38, 40, 45, 59, 91
♿ Good
✋ Free

HIGHLIGHTS

Ajuntament
● Original medieval side façade
● Courtyard sculptures by Miró, Gargallo, Subirachs
● Tiles with craft implements (Saló de Cent)
● Saló de Croniques with historic murals by Sert

Generalitat
● The orange tree patio
● Chapel of St. George

The *sardana* danced here every Sunday at midday is one expression of Catalan culture; other symbols of Catalan identity are the palaces facing each other across the square, the Generalitat and the Ajuntament.

Provincial parliament The *plaça*, for centuries the site of a church and a cemetery, is one of the focal points of city life. Here demonstrations and processions wind up and many a historic speech has been made. The Palau de la Generalitat, on the north side of the square, is the home of the regional government, successor to the Corts Catalanes of the medieval kingdom of Catalonia and Aragon. Begun in the 14th century, the building housing the Palau de la Generalitat has several features celebrating St. George, patron saint of Catalonia; the chapel is named after him, and there's a medieval George over the 15th-century façade on Carrer Bisbe and a more modern George on the frontage overlooking the square. Generalitat is open to the public 10.30–1.30 on the second and fourth Sunday of each month.

City Hall The Ajuntament, or Casa de la Ciutat, is the seat of city government. Beyond the 19th-century main façade, the courtyard retains the feeling of a medieval palace. Stairways lead to an open gallery off which opens the exquisite 14th-century Saló de Cent (Room of the Hundred). From here, the semi-democratic Consell de Cent (Council of the Hundred) ruled Barcelona like a city-state for nearly five centuries.

Fans for sale in one of the Barri Gòtic's many specialist shops

Shopping in the Barri Gòtic

Barcelona's Barri Gòtic, the oldest part of the city, is a dense maze of shops, cafés, alleyways and squares. You'll find antiques dealers, galleries and gourmet food stores side by side with quirky boutiques and fast-food outlets.

North of the Plaça del Pí Start at the corner of the Ramblas and the Carrer de la Portaferrissa. Portaferrissa is one of the barri's busiest shopping streets, with a wide selection of cheap and cheerful fashion stores aimed squarely at the young. Walk down and take the second right onto Carrer de Petritxol where clothes shops give way to chic galleries selling antiques and pictures, including landscapes and city scenes of Catalonia and Barcelona. At the end of Petritxol you'll find yourself in picturesque Plaça del Pí. The adjoining Plaça de Sant Josep Oriol has an art market every Saturday and some good home textile shops. Several good shopping streets branch off the square. Take Carrer de la Palla to track down food specialties and some wonderfully old-fashioned toy stores.

South of the Plaça del Pí Alternatively, take Carrer de l'Ave Maria out of Oriol and turn left onto the top section of Carrer dels Banys Nous. Here you'll find boutiques concentrating on beads and dress jewellery, lovely bags and carnival costumes and kids' dressing-up outfits. Heading south; there's a splendid old-fashioned hat shop at the junction with Carrer de la Palla and more trinket and jewellery shops along the Carrer Boqueria.

THE BASICS

➕ G7–G8
🚇 Liceu, Catalunya
🚌 14, 38, 59, 91

HIGHLIGHTS

● Browsing at the weekend markets
● An outside table at the Bar del Pí on the Plaça del Pí is the perfect place for people-watching
● Recharge your energy with a sugar fix at any of the *granjas* (cake and coffee shops) along the Carrer Petrixol. Try a *suizo*: a thick hot chocolate topped with whipped cream

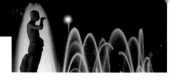

More to See

LA BOQUERIA

Barcelona's central market is a city landmark. Although the official name is Mercat de Sant Josep, it is better known as La Boqueria (the butchery). This superb iron-and-glass market hall was built in the 19th century to house the food stands that cluttered up the Rambla and its surrounding streets. Beyond the market's gaping arch, are countless stands piled high with every foodstuff from the Mediterranean and its Catalonian hinterland.

✚ G7 ✉ Rambla 91 ☎ 93 318 25 84
Ⓜ Liceu

DE LA MERCÈ

Together with St. Eulàlia, Our Lady of Mercy is one of Barcelona's patron saints. Her church, one of the finest baroque buildings in the city, was erected in the 1760s, replacing a much earlier building.

✚ G8 ✉ Plaça de la Mercè Ⓜ Drassanes

MUSEU DE CERA

www.museocerabcn.com

Housed in a lovely 19th-century stately building, the wax museum in the Rambla is charmingly old-fashioned, though a real kids-pleaser.

✚ G8 ✉ Passatge de la Banca 7 ☎ 93 317 26 49 🕒 Jul–end Sep, daily 10–10; Oct–end Jun, Mon–Fri 10–1.30, 4–7.30; weekends and hols 11–2, 4.30–8.30 ✋ Moderate
Ⓜ Drassanes

MUSEU FREDERIC MARÈS

www.museumares.bcn.es

There are three main reasons for visiting this museum named after the long-lived sculptor and obsessive collector Frederic Marès: its setting overlooking the courtyard garden of the Royal Palace; its inexhaustible collection of sculpture from pre-Roman times to the 19th century; and last (but far from least), the section known as the Collecciò Sentimental (Sentimental Museum), with its surreal array of everyday objects from the 15th to the 19th centuries.

✚ G7 ✉ Plaça Sant Iu 5 ☎ 93 310 58 00
🕒 Tue–Sat 10–7, Sun 10–3 🍴 Café
Ⓜ Jaume I ♿ Few ✋ Moderate. Free first Sun of month and Wed 3–7

The top façade of de la Mercè (above)

Detail of a mother and child statue in the Museu Frederic Marès (right)

PLAÇA DE CATALUNYA

City life seems to revolve around this spacious central square, not least because of its position at the upper end of the Ramblas. The main landmark is the huge slablike Corte Inglès department store; it is also the location of the largest tourist office and the principal transport stop-off. You can catch a bus or train connection to anywhere in town, including the airport. The number of monuments and statues is considerable and well worth a look. A 1991 addition commemorates the popular pre-Civil War politician Francesc Macià.

✚ G7 🚇 Catalunya

PLAÇA DEL PÍ

Set amid the warren of winding streets between the cathedral and the Ramblas you'll find Plaça del Pí and the adjoining Plaça Sant Josep, two of Barcelona's most beguiling squares. These asymmetrical spaces have leafy shade, laid-back cafés and weekend art exhibitions, a great place to relax. Pí is named for the pine trees that

once grew here, as is the serene church, Santa Maria del Pí. The monumentally plain exterior of this Barri Gòtic church conceals an equally austere interior—a single nave in characteristic Catalan Gothic style. The main façade, its statues long since gone, has a fine rose window. The octagonal bell tower is 55m (180ft) high.

✚ G7/8 🕐 Church: weekdays 8.30–1, 4.30–9; otherwise 8–2, 5–9 🚇 Liceu

PLAÇA REIAL

With its arcades and classical façades, this grandiose and splendidly symmetrical square is in complete contrast to the crooked streets and alleyways of the surrounding Barri Gòtic. Built in the mid-19th century on the model of the squares of Paris, it is a preferred hangout of idlers and winos, though it is considerably smarter than it once was. Antoni Gaudí designed the sinuous, wrought-iron lampposts, his first official commission by the city of Barcelona in the 1870s.

✚ G8 🚇 Liceu

The arcaded oasis of the Plaça Reial

The Barri Gòtic

A stroll round the heart of the Barri Gòtic that takes you past some of its main sights.

DISTANCE: 1.5km (1 mile) **ALLOW:** 45–60 minutes

START

END

PLAÇA DE L'ÀNGEL ✚ G8
🚇 Jaume I

PLAÇA DE L'ÀNGEL
🚇 Jaume I

① With your back to the large thoroughfare, Via Laietana, look for the road to your right, Baixada de la Llibreteria. Walk along to the intersection with Carrer de Veguer. Turn right.

⑧ Turn right where the road name changes to Carrer de la Dagueria. At the intersection with Carrer de la Jaume I, turn right. The Plaça de l'Àngel, where you started, is on the left. The metro station, Jaume I, is also here.

② Walk to the end to the Plaça del Rei. With your back to the Plaça, take the right-hand exit onto Baixada de Santa Clara. You then come to the rear of the cathedral.

⑦ Continue down Carrer del Regomir then turn left onto Carrer del Correu Vell. In a few steps the street becomes Carrer de Lledó. Continue ahead past Plaça de Sant Just.

③ Turn right along Carrer dels Comtes (the cathedral is on your left). Continue ahead, pass the Museu Frederic Marès and continue on to the Plaça de la Seu.

⑥ Turn left onto Carrer del Call and continue to the immense Plaça de Sant Jaume. Bear right and take Carrer de la Ciutat, which eventually becomes Carrer del Regomir.

④ Take an immediate left onto Carrer de Santa Llùcia. Turn left onto Carrer de Bisbe and then turn hard right onto the winding Montjuïc del Bisbe to the square of Sant Felip Neri.

⑤ Take the farthest exit out of the square onto Carrer de Sant Felip Neri. Turn left onto Carrer de Sant Domenech del Call.

Shopping

LAS RAMBLAS AND THE BARRI GÒTIC

ALAMACENES DE PILAR

For combs, shawls, fans feathers, and all Spanish finery, this large shop has the best selection. Items include spotted flamenco dresses and bolts of silk brocade. Prices range from a few euros for a wooden fan, or hundreds for a richly embroidered silk mantilla (shawl).

✚ G8 ✉ Carrer Boqueria 43 ☎ 93 317 79 84 Ⓜ Liceu

ART ESCUDELLERS

If it's local ceramics or glassware you are after, this is the place. Wares are laid out by region, from the simple terracotta and green pottery of Catalonia to more intricate, hand-painted tiles and other ceramics from Valencia and Andalucia. One-off pieces from local artists are also available. Despite its touristy look, prices are reasonable.

✚ G8 ✉ Carrer Escudellers 23 ☎ 93 412 68 01 Ⓜ Drassanes

BARRI GÒTIC ANTIQUES MARKET

Bric-à-brac rather than heirloom bargains dominate the stands in front of the cathedral.

✚ G7 ✉ Avinguda de la Catedral 6 ☎ 93 291 61 18 🕐 Thu 9–8 Ⓜ Jaume I

LE BOUDOIR

Luxuriously silk and satin underwear, lingerie and swimwear are on sale in this lovely shop, which is decorated in the style of a *fin de siècle* French salon with gilt mirrors and over-size velvet pillows. Also discreet sex toys and a erotic books, all that tease rather than shock.

✚ G7 ✉ Carrer Canuda 21 ☎ 93 302 52 81 Ⓜ Liceu

CAELUM

All over Spain nuns in their convents produce delicious cakes, biscuits and sweets, make candles, scented soap and exquisite embroidery. Caelum stocks such delights from all over the country, beautifully and traditionally packaged, and there's a café to sample before you buy.

✚ G7 ✉ Carrer de la Palla 8 ☎ 93 302 69 93 Ⓜ Liceu, Jaume I

CERERIA SUBIRÁ

Dating from 1761, this shop is supposedly the oldest in the city. Started

WHAT TO BUY IN THE BARRI GÒTIC

The intricate streets and alleyways of the old town east of the Rambla are full of individual shops selling virtually everything you might want to either eat or admire. There are craftsmen's candles, cured hams and all kinds of antiques and art objects. Portaferrissa and Portal de l'Angel streets have fashion boutiques and shoe shops.

as a ladies outfitters, it now sells candles in all shapes and sizes. The staff, with their starched uniforms, seem to come from another era.

✚ G8 ✉ Baixada de Llibreteria 7 ☎ 93 315 26 06 Ⓜ Jaume I

LA COLMENA

Cakes of all description, biscuits and sweets in this traditional shop.

✚ G8 ✉ Plaça de l'Àngel 12 ☎ 93 315 13 56 Ⓜ Jaume I

EL CORTE INGLÉS

Virtually everything you could ever need under the roof of an aircraft-carrier-like establishment. On the several floors between the supermarket in the basement and the eating place at the top are designer fashions, cosmetics, jewels, handicrafts, a stationery shop, a bookshop, a travel bureau and an interpreter service.

✚ G7 ✉ Plaça de Catalunya 14 ☎ 93 306 38 00 Ⓜ Catalunya

COSES DE CASA

This fabulous, wood-panel shop in pretty Plaça Sant Josep Orol specializes in unusual upholstery fabrics, featuring ethnic-inspired prints, weaves and embroidery. Some are made up into take-home goodies such as toiletry bags, cushion covers and gorgeous throws.

✚ G7 ✉ Plaça Sant Josep Oriol 5 ☎ 93 302 73 28 Ⓜ Liceu

FORMATGERIA LA SEU
This shop is dedicated to Spanish and Catalan cheeses. Pop in for a tasting with wine, before stocking up on hard-to-get treats to take home.
➕ G8 ✉ Carrer de la Dagueria 16 ☎ 93 412 65 48 Ⓜ Jaume 1

GANIVETERIA ROCA
If you're looking for the perfect knife, shears, scissors, penknife or blade of any type, this long-established store has one of the largest ranges in Europe; it also offers a sharpening service.
➕ G7 ✉ Plaça del Pí 3 ☎ 93 302 12 41 Ⓜ Liceu, Jaume I

GOTHAM
Restored furniture and an eclectic selection of lamps from the 1950s, '60s, and '70s, as well as many art deco pieces.
➕ G8 ✉ Cervantes 7 ☎ 93 412 46 47 Ⓜ Jaume I

EL INGENIO
Even if you are not in the market for a carnival costume, this shop will delight. El Ingenio is like stepping into a giant dress-up box, with a cornucopia of costumes, masks, wigs and party tricks and novelties. At the back there are some *capgrosses* on display (papier mâché heads that are marched out during the city's celebrations).
➕ G8 ✉ Carrer Rauric 6 ☎ 93 317 71 38 Ⓜ Liceu

JOGUINES MONFORTE
This superbly traditional shop specializes in old-fashioned board games for adults and kids, as well as jigsaw puzzles, wooden solitaire boards and chess sets. Snap up a game of *parchís* (ludo) or *el juego del oca* (the goose game), a Spanish-style snakes and ladders.
➕ G7 ✉ Plaça Sant Josep Oriol 3 ☎ 93 318 22 85 Ⓜ Liceu

LA MANUAL ALPARGATERA
All kinds of woven items, some created before your eyes. The specialty: hand-made espadrilles.
➕ G8 ✉ Carrer d'Avinyó 7 ☎ 93 301 01 72 Ⓜ Liceu

PAPABUBBLE
Kids will adore this concept candy shop, where the goodies are made on the spot, so you can watch them roll, twist and form the soft candy into unusual shapes, and have them personalize it for

you. The tastes are as unique as the packaging; ask to try the flower and cocktail combinations.
➕ G8 ✉ Carrer Ample 28 ☎ 93 268 86 25 Ⓜ Jaume I

PLAÇA REIAL: COIN AND STAMP MARKET
The Plaça Reial plays host every Sunday to stand-holders and collector types indulging their enthusiasms.
➕ G8 ✉ Plaça Reial 🕐 Sun 9–2.30 Ⓜ Liceu

PLAÇA DE SANT JOSEP ORIOL: PICTURE MARKET
This art market takes place in one of the Barri Gòtic's most picturesque squares. Worth a browse.
➕ G7 ✉ Plaça de Sant Josep Oriol 🕐 Sun 9–6 Ⓜ Liceu

SALA PARÉS
The city's best art gallery, showing works of leading Catalan artists.
➕ G8 ✉ Petrixol 5 ☎ 93 318 70 20 Ⓜ Liceu

EL TRIANGLE
This complex contains, among other shops, FNAC and Habitat. FNAC is one of the city's best sources for books, with a large English section, videos and CDs. The perfume and cosmetics shop, Sephora is also here, and there is a branch of the fashion chain Massimo Dutti.
➕ G7 ✉ Plaça de Catalunya 4 ☎ 93 318 01 08 Ⓜ Catalunya

Entertainment and Nightlife

DOT LIGHT CLUB
A small, trendy night club behind the Plaça Reial, with an intimate bar area and a dance floor where a top sound system delivers everything from chill-out electronic to house.
➕ G8 ✉ Carrer Nou de Sant Francesc 7 ☎ 93 302 70 26 🕐 Tue–Thu 11pm–2am, Fri–Sun 9pm–2am 🚇 Drassanes

FONFONE
A 1980s-feel dominates this bar-club, from the green neon lighting to the red dance floor and slot-car racing tracks adorning the walls. Electro beats match the decor, and on Thursday nights the tracks turn to classic funk.
➕ G8 ✉ Escudellers 25 ☎ 93 317 14 24 🕐 Daily 10pm–3am 🚇 Drassanes

GRAN TEATRE DEL LICEU
Destroyed by fire in 1861, rebuilt, then burned again in 1994, the Lyceum holds a special place in the hearts of musical Barcelonins, since it was here that the city's passion for opera found its prime expression. The rebuilt Liceu occupies an block on the Lower Rambla and the opera is back!
➕ G8 ✉ Rambla 61–65 ☎ 93 485 99 13 🚇 Liceu

HARLEM JAZZ CLUB
Barcelona's oldest jazz club has certainly moved with the times and still packs in the crowds who come to enjoy some of the most varied music in the city—everything from jazz to flamenco fusion.
➕ G8 ✉ Carrer de la Comtessa de Sobradiel 8 ☎ 93 310 07 55 🕐 Closed Sun and Mon 🚇 Jaume I

JAMBOREE
An underground jazz club that's almost cavelike, hosting blues, soul, jazz, funk and occasional hip-hop live bands. At 1am on weekends, the dance floor opens and gets crowded quite quickly. Upstairs is Los Tarantos, a bar with predominantly Spanish music.
➕ G8 ✉ Plaça Reial 17 ☎ 93 301 75 64 🕐 Daily 9pm–5am 🚇 Liceu

KARMA
This basement venue is still the most popular of several lively rock clubs around Plaça Reial.

NIGHT ZONES
Vigorous nightlife takes place all over the city. Plaça Reial in the old town is always active, though new laws on noise levels have pushed many late-night clubs out of the inner city and into the suburbs, where the action takes place until dawn and beyond. The Eixample area has plenty of classy cocktail bars and summer terraces with some of the smoother venues on the exclusive slopes of the wealthy suburb of Tibidabo.

➕ G9 ✉ Plaça Reial 10 ☎ 93 302 56 80 🕐 Tue–Sun midnight–5am 🚇 Liceu

LA MACARENA
This tiny techno club in the back streets of the Barri Gòtic pulls in plenty of punters post 2am. International DJs regularly play here, and the minis-cule dance floor gets jam packed. Expect to queue.
➕ G8 ✉ Carrer Nou de Sant Francesc 5 ☎ 93 302 45 93 🕐 Mon–Sat midnight–5am 🚇 Drassanes

MALDÀ
One of Barcelona's best-loved institutions, this inti-mate little cinema reopened after a major face-lift in 2005. It screens independent film and Asian cinema.
➕ G7 ✉ Carrer del Pí 5 ☎ 93 481 37 04 🚇 Liceu

NEW YORK
This rock club has had a recent face-lift and now hosts great *musica negra* nights, when locals flock to dance to everything from northern soul to funk.
➕ G8 ✉ Carrer d'Escudellers 5 ☎ 93 318 87 30 🕐 Thu–Sat midnight–5am 🚇 Liceu

LOS TARANTOS
Here you will find some of the best flamenco acts in Catalonia. Conveniently located in Plaça Reial. You can dine while watching. Most gigs start at 10pm.
➕ G8 ✉ Plaça Reial 17 ☎ 93 301 75 64 🚇 Liceu

Restaurants

PRICES

Prices are approximate, based on a 3-course meal for one person.

€€€	over €50
€€	€25–€50
€	under €25

AGUT (€€)

The Agut family, which has owned and managed the restaurant for the last three generations, has a menu reflecting seasonal availability as well as dishes that are popular all year round, such as *olla barrejada* (a typical Catalan stew with vegetables an meat) and *fideuà* (fish noodles), cod with red peppers and garlic mayonnaise.

🔲 G8 ✉ Carrer d'en Gignàs 16 ☎ 93 315 17 09 🕐 Tue–Sat 1.30–4, 9–12, Sun 1–4; closed Aug 🚇 Jaume I

BAR DEL PÍ (€)

Friendly service at this *tapas* bar delightfully located in the little square dominated by the church of Santa Maria del Pí.

🔲 G7 ✉ Place Sant Josep Oriol 🕐 Closed Mon 🚇 Liceu

LA BODEGA DE PALMA (€)

This rustic, old-school *tapas* bar is equally as popular with locals as visitors. Get here around 8.30pm to grab one of the tiny marble tables and order marinated sardines and homemade

omelette or share a plate of stuffed peppers over a jug of barrel wine. Service is tourist-friendly without being touristy.

🔲 G8 ✉ Carrer Palma de Sant Just 7 ☎ 93 315 06 56 🕐 Mon–Fri 8.30am–11pm, Sat 11am–11.30pm 🚇 Jaume I

CAFÉ DE L'ACADEMIA (€€)

Not really a café at all, this restaurant offers some of the best deals in town on a variety of traditional Mediterranean cuisine. Reserve ahead.

🔲 G8 ✉ Carrer de Lledó 1, Ciutat Vella ☎ 93 315 00 26 🕐 Closed weekends, hols 🚇 Jaume I

CAFÉ DE L'OPERA (€)

Opera goers and tourists fill the art nouveau interior and terrace tables of this dignified establishment opposite the Liceu. A great place for a spot of people-watching on the Rambla, but the coffees, drinks and snacks don't

GALICIAN FLAVOURS

Many restaurants in Barcelona specialize in Galician cuisine. Galicia, the northwest region of Spain, is famous for its seafood—octopus, crab, scallops, clams and sardines are all simply prepared and delicious. Traditional Galician country fare is also excellent; try *empanadas* (pastry filled with seafood or meat).

come cheap.

🔲 G8 ✉ Rambla 74 ☎ 93 317 75 85 🕐 Daily 🚇 Liceu

CAN CULLERETES (€€)

Can Culleretes has the distinction of being one of the oldest restaurants in Barcelona, founded in 1786 as a pastry shop. The menu is like a catalogue of old-fashioned Catalan cuisine, but there are modern dishes, too. Sample the *botifarra* (pork sausage) with white beans.

🔲 G8 ✉ Carrer d'en Quintana 5, Ciutat Vella ☎ 93 317 64 85 🕐 Closed Sun evening, Mon, Jul 🚇 Liceu

JUICY JONES (€)

A hot spot for vegetarians, this well-established juice bar churns out every combination of juices and smoothies, as well as filled baguettes, Indian rice, couscous dishes and elaborate salads—and it's all fresh and vegan-friendly.

🔲 G8 ✉ Carrer del Cardenal Casañas 7 ☎ 93 302 43 30 🕐 Daily 🚇 Liceu

KYNOTO (€€)

This stylish sushi restaurant also offers unusual cocktails and free Wi-Fi.

🔲 G8 ✉ Carrer Correu Vell 8 ☎ 93 268 25 40 🕐 Mon–Sat 9pm–2am 🚇 Jaume I

LA LOCANDA (€€)

This stylish Italian restaurant by the cathedral offers great pizzas fresh from the wood-fired oven as well as a select choice of pastas, risottos, gnocchi, carpaccios and salads. Recommended is the *arroz con ceps* (wild mushroom risotto) and their creamy lasagne.

➕ G7 ✉ Carrer Doctor Joaquim Pou 4 ☎ 93 317 46 09 🕐 Closed Monday 🚇 Jaume I

PITARRA (€)

Pitarra, a traditional Catalan restaurant, has no shortage of character. It was named after Serafí Pitarra, a famous Catalan actor and former resident. The cuisine is excellent, particularly the cannelloni and the seasonal highlights, notably the mushroom-based dishes. Service is attentive.

➕ G8 ✉ Carrer d'Avinyó 56 ☎ 93 301 16 47 🕐 Daily; closed Aug 🚇 Drassanes

PLA (€€)

An excellent spot for a romantic meal in the Barri Gòtic, within walking distance of the town hall on Plaça de Sant Jaume. The chef draws on the influences of Mediterranean, vegetarian and international cooking. There's a wide selection of carpaccio: fish with prawns, beef with pineapple vinaigrette, and veal with liver. The crêpes with nuts and the sautéed vegetables with chicken are good, but a house special is the tuna *tataki* with lime leaves in a citrus and coconut sauce, presented on a banana leaf.

➕ G8 ✉ Carrer de Bellafila 5 ☎ 93 412 65 52 🕐 Dinner only daily 🚇 Jaume I

ELS QUATRE GATS (€€)

The Four Cats was frequented by Barcelona's turn-of-the-century bohemian crowd (including Picasso), two of whom are depicted in the famous picture (a reproduction) of arty types riding a tandem bicycle. There is a bar up front, while the restaurant is situated in the back.

➕ G7 ✉ Montsío 3bis

CATALAN COOKING

Catalonia is generally reckoned to have one of the great regional cuisines of Spain. It is based on good ingredients from the varied countryside and on seafood from the Mediterranean and the Atlantic. Four principal sauces are used. There is *sofregit* (onion, tomato and garlic cooked in olive oil); with added sweet pepper, aubergine and courgette it becomes *samfaina*. *Picada* is made by pounding nuts, fried bread, parsley, saffron and other ingredients in a mortar. Finally there is garlic mayonnaise, *alioli*.

☎ 93 302 41 40 🕐 Daily 🚇 Urquinaona, Catalunya

TALLER DE TAPAS (€)

Unashamedly aimed at tourists wanting to try *tapas* but wary of ordering across the counter, this sleek *tapas* bar has multilingual menus and plenty of seating—the *tapas* is excellent, particularly the seafood and vegetable dishes.

➕ G7 ✉ Plaça de Sant Josep Oriol 9 ☎ 93 301 80 20 🕐 Daily 🚇 Liceu

TAXIDERMISTA (€€)

Taxidermista overlooks the city's liveliest square. The interior is bright and rather Parisian in style, and it has become a meeting spot for an international crowd. The menu is comprehensive, light and presented, well with local market cuisine and *tapas*.

➕ G8 ✉ Plaça Reial 8 ☎ 93 412 45 36 🕐 Tue–Sun 12–4, 8.30–12.30 🚇 Liceu

VINATERIA DEL CALL (€)

This low-ceilinged, Gothic-looking bodega is perceived to be one of the best places to taste *pa amb tomaquèt*, the ubiquitous Catalan 'tomato bread' (▷ 38). Try it with all sorts of cheese and charcuterie, accompanied by a glass of rioja from their excellent wine list.

➕ G8 ✉ C. Sant Domenec del Call 9 ☎ 93 302 60 92 🕐 Dinner only; closed Sun 🚇 Liceu

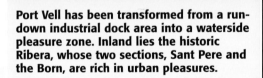

Port Vell and La Ribera

Port Vell has been transformed from a run-down industrial dock area into a waterside pleasure zone. Inland lies the historic Ribera, whose two sections, Sant Pere and the Born, are rich in urban pleasures.

5

6

7

8

9

G   H

Carrer   de   Girona   Casp
Carrer   DEL   BRUC
Casa Calvet
Carrer   d'Ausiàs
CARRER DE BAILÈN
PASSEIG DE SANT JOAN
RONDA   DE   Carrer
CARRER   DE   SANT   PERE
TRAFALGAR
Arc de Triomf
CARRER   DE   Arc del Triomf
Palau de la Música Catalana
Plaça St Pere
CASC ANTIC
Carrer Sant Pere Mitjà
Carrer Sant Pere més Baix
C Cortines
A F Cambó
C Girafí
C. Portal Nou
PASSEIG
LLUÍS COMPANYS
Mercat Santa Caterina
Carrers
C Metges
Carrer del Comerç
Museu de Zoologia
Museu de Xocolata
PICASSO
CARRER   DE   LA   PRINCESA
Museu de Geologia
Museu Tèxtil i d'Indumentària
Museu Picasso
PASSEIG DE
Museu Barbier-Mueller d'Art Precolombí
Passeig del Born
Carrer de Comercial
Mercat del Born
VIA LAIETANA
Santa Maria del Mar
Plaça del Born
RIBERA
Carrer de Consolat de Mar
La Llotja
Plaça del Palau
AVINGUDA MARQUÈS DE L'ARGENTERA
PASSEIG DE
PLAÇA D'ANTONI LÓPEZ
PG ISABEL II
ESTACIÓ BARCELONA DE FRANÇA

0   250 m
0   250 yds

Moll de Bosch i Alsina
Barceloneta
CARRER DEL DR AIGUADER
Palau de Mar
Plaça de Pau Vila
RONDA
Museu d'Història de Catalunya
CARRER DEL DR AIGUADER
Dàrsena Nacional
Moll d'Espanya
Carrer   Balboa
LITORAL
Carrer de Ginebra
Carrer del
Carrer de Sant
PASSEIG DE JOAN DE BORBÓ
Parc de Barcelona
Dàrsena del Comerç
Plaça Barceloneta
Plaça de Pompeu Fabra
PG del
Reial Club Marítim
Plaça de la Font
Moll de la Barceloneta
C d'Andrea Dòria
Poliesport Marítim
Port Vell
L'Aquàrium
BARCELONETA
Carrer   Sant   Carles
Carrer Almirall Cervera
Plaça Brugada
PASSEIG
San Miquel del Port
Platja

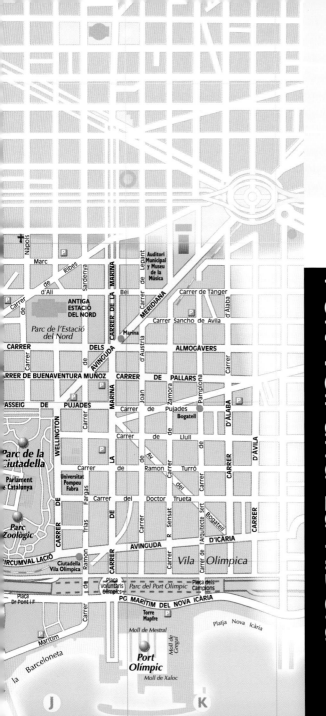

Port Vell and La Ribera

Barceloneta

The popular beach at Barceloneta (left) and a fish sculpture (right)

THE BASICS

➕ H/J9
✉ Barceloneta
Ⓜ Barceloneta
🚌 17, 39, 45, 57, 64, 157
❓ Barceloneta's Festa
Major, with music, parades, dancing on the beach and fireworks runs through the 3rd week in Sept

HIGHLIGHTS

● Plaça Barceloneta with baroque church of San Miquel del Port (▷ 72)
● The Mercet de Barceloneta
● Market on Plaça de la Font
● Passeig Marítim
● The beaches

The cramped streets of Barceloneta evoke the culture of a traditional Mediterranean fishing village. Cut off from the rest of the city for years, this vibrant area has its own atmosphere and identity.

Little Barcelona Displaced by the building of the Ciutadella (▷ 66), many people from the Ribera moved to live in shanty dwellings between the port and the sea. In 1751 the shacks were swept away, the land was reclaimed, and this new triangular district, Barceloneta, was developed. Designed by French army engineer, Prosper Verboom, it comprises long narrow blocks of identical housing, the regularity broken by squares. By the 19th century the *barri* had become the traditional home of dock workers and fishermen, divided from the rest of the city after the construction of a rail-and-road barrier at one end.

Moves of change During the 1990s, the whole of the Port Vell (▷ 68–69) was redeveloped, and the northern end of Passeig Joan de Borbó, became a smart waterfront promenade and marina. The famous *chiringuitos*, basic but wonderful seafood restaurants that once lined the waterfront, were swept away and the beach added and its surroundings landscaped. Barceloneta itself has undergone something of a transformation, with a new market, more housing and Benedetta Tagliabue's glittering glass-faced Natural Gas building. The *barri's* symbol has become Estel Ferit (wounded star), a sculpture of three stacked cubes on the beach.

The exterior of the museum (left and middle) and a painting from Las Meninas *(right)*

Museu Picasso

Picasso, the greatest painter of modern times, came to live in Barcelona at the age of 14. Many of his formative experiences took place in the old town and a museum devoted to his work is here.

Picasso's palace The Picasso Museum's collection concentrates on certain periods of Picasso's life and artistic evolution, including his time in Barcelona. The work benefits enormously from its setting; the magnificent Palau Berenguer d'Aguilar and four adjacent buildings give an excellent idea of the lifestyle enjoyed by the merchant families at the height of medieval Barcelona's prosperity.

At home and away An Andalucian hailing from Malaga, Pablo Ruiz Picasso accompanied his art teacher father and family to Barcelona in 1895. His skills flourished at his father's academy and later, at art school in Madrid. Beginning in 1899, he immersed himself in bohemian Barcelona, frequenting the red-light district centred on Carrer d'Avinyó, the inspiration for *Demoiselles d'Avignon* (1907). He became a habitué of Els Quatre Gats (Four Cats, ▷ 58), a café whose menu he designed. His first exhibition was held here in 1900, the year he made his first visit to Paris. France was to be his real home after that, but he returned to Barcelona many times, and much of the work in his Blue Period (*c*1902–04) was carried out here. The Civil War, which provoked one of his most passionate paintings, *Guernica*— now in the Centro Nacional de Arte Reina Sofía in Madrid—put an end to these visits.

THE BASICS

www.museupicasso.bcn.es
✚ H8
✉ Carrer Montcada 15–23
☎ 93 315 01 02
🕐 Tue–Sat 10–8, Sun 10–3. Closed 1 Jan, 1 May, 24 Jun, 25 and 26 Dec
🍴 Café-restaurant
Ⓜ Jaume I
🚌 17, 19, 40, 45
♿ Good
🎫 Moderate; free 11 Feb, 18 May, 24 Sep

HIGHLIGHTS

● Ceramics from 1940s and 1950s
● *The Embrace* (1900)
● *Science and Charity* (1897)
● *La Nana* (The Dwarf), 1901
● *El Loco* (The Madman), 1904
● *Harlequin* (1917)
● *Las Meninas* suite (1957)
● Cannes paintings of landscapes and doves (late 1950s)

Palau de la Música Catalana

The elaborate exterior of the concert hall (left) and the interior (right)

THE BASICS

www.palaumusica.org

⊞ H7

✉ Carrer Sant Francesc de Paula 2

☎ 90 244 28 82

🕐 Guided visits daily 10–3.30

🍴 Bar

Ⓜ Urquinaona

🚌 17, 19, 40, 45

♿ Good

💲 Expensive (tickets in advance from gift shop)

HIGHLIGHTS

Main façade
- Catalan songsters in mosaic
- Composers' busts
- Proscenium sculpture *Allegory of Catalan Folksong*
- Foyer vaults with floral capitals
- Lluís Millet Room
- Bust of Pau (Pablo) Casals (given 1936)
- Modern statue of Millet conducting (outside new entrance)

For nearly a century, this glittering jewel has served not only as a concert hall but also as an icon of Catalan cultural life. The profusion of ornament is staggering—a delight in itself.

Catalan icon The sumptuous Palace of Catalan Music was designed by the great *modernista* architect Domènech i Montaner as the home of the Catalan national choir, the Orfeó. It was inaugurated in 1908 to unanimous acclaim and became a symbol of the new renaissance in Catalan culture. Montaner gave the building a steel frame to support profuse interior and exterior decoration intended to inspire and instruct. This decoration was the work of his own ceramicists, painters, glassworkers and tilers.

Art-full auditorium Riches encrust the main façade, the entrance hall, the foyer and staircase, but the 2,000-seat concert hall is even more ornate. Light pours in through the transparent walls and from the roof, from which hangs an extraordinary bowl of stained glass. The proscenium arch, far from being a static frame, seems to swell and move, such is the dynamism of its pale pumice sculptures. On the left, a willow tree shelters the great mid-19th-century reviver of Catalan music, Josep Anselm Clavé; on the right a bust of Beethoven is upstaged by Wagnerian Valkyries rollicking through the clouds. Equally stunning is the curving wall at the back of the stage, from which emerge the 18 Muses of music. Reserve in advance for a performance.

Fish restaurants at the Palau de Mar (left) and Museu d'Història de Catalunya (right)

Palau de Mar

Dispel any ignorance of Catalonia's past with a visit to the entertaining Palau de Mar, home to the Museu d'Historia de Catalunya. Innovative and interactive exhibits clarify what has gone into the creation of this nation within a nation.

Catalonia! Catalonia! An imposing late 19th-century warehouse houses this stimulating museum. Although Catalan history may be something of a mystery to casual visitors, it's worth knowing more about—the past speaks volumes about the present and current aspirations. General Franco wanted Catalan identity to disappear altogether; the museum is one of many initiatives that the regional government (the Generalitat) took to restore it. The exhibits are exclusively in Catalan, but many are self-explanatory, and Spanish and English summaries are available.

Intriguing exhibits The waterfront museum highlights themes from history in a series of spaces grouped around a central atrium. There are few objects on display, but exhibits are truly ingenious; you can work an Arab waterwheel, walk over a skeleton in its shallow grave, climb on to a cavalier's charger and test the weight of his armour, enter a medieval forest, peer into a primitive stone cabin, enjoy a driver's-eye view from an early tram, and cower in a Civil War air-raid shelter. Sound effects, films and interactive screens enhance the experience and the temporary shows, which deal with aspects of Catalonia's history, are of a very high standard.

THE BASICS

www.mhcat.net
🏠 H9
✉ Plaça de Pau Vila 3
☎ 93 225 47 00
🕐 Tue, Thu–Sat 10–7, Wed 10–8, Sun 10–2.30
🍴 Café
Ⓜ Barceloneta
🚌 14, 17, 39, 57, 59, 64
♿ Good
💷 Moderate

HIGHLIGHTS

● Early ship packed with amphorae
● Moorish market stall
● Sinister Civil Guards pursuing insurgents
● Civil War machine-gun emplacement
● Franco-era schoolroom
● 1930s kitchen with objects to handle
● First edition of George Orwell's *Homage to Catalonia*
● 1960s tourist bar with *Speak Inglis/Parle Frances* sign

Parc de la Ciutadella

Steps leading to the park (left) and the Arc de Triomf (right)

THE BASICS

➕ H/J8

🅰 Arc de Triomf, Barceloneta, Ciutadella

🚌 14, 39, 41, 59

HIGHLIGHTS

● Hivernacle conservatory
● Umbracle conservatory
● Castle of three dragons (Zoological Museum)

Sculptures

● *Sorrow* by Josep Llimona
● *Lady with Parasol* by Joan Roig, 1884 (in Zoo)
● *Homage to Picasso* by A Tàpies (1983) (on Passeig de Picasso)

In the 1860s and 1870s the great Citadel, a symbol of Bourbon oppression, was demolished. In its place, the city laid out its first public park, still a shady haven on the edge of the city hub.

The Citadel Covering an area almost as big as the city itself at the time, the monstrous Citadel was built to cow the Catalans after their defeat on 11 September, 1714, by the new Bourbon monarch of Spain, Philip V. A garrison of 8,000 troops kept the population in check, and the Citadel was loathed as a place where local patriots were executed. In 1868, the Catalan General Juan Prim y Prats came to power and ordered its demolition, a process already begun by the enthusiastic citizens.

The park today The public park that took the Citadel's place (and name) shows little trace of the great fortress, though the Arsenal houses the Catalan Parliament. Other structures are leftovers from the Universal Expo of 1888: an ornate Arc de Triomf (Triumphal Arch), and a fairy tale, *modernista* restaurant designed by Domènech i Montaner and now home to the Zoological Museum. The zoo itself is to the south (▷ 72), while the Geology Museum is in the northern flank. Throughout the park, fine trees and shrubs and a boating lake soften the formal layout. The imposing Font Monumental, an extraordinary fountain feature, incorporates just about every allegorical element possible and was worked on by Gaudí, then an architecture student.

The marina at Port Olímpic (left) and stealing some shade at a café (right)

Port Olímpic and the Beaches

The eye-catching development of the Vila Olímpica, built for the 1992 Olympic Games, is a stunning ensemble of marinas, broad promenades, glittering buildings and open space.

Port Olímpic The marina is the heart of the new Olympic district, built as the focus of the water events, and backed by the apartments, which once housed the athletes. Sleek and expensive yachts and boats of all shapes and sizes line the pontoons. The enclosed marina, and the nearby promenades, are lined with bars and restaurants of all descriptions. Inland, the tallest buildings are the Mapfre towers and the opulent Hotel Arts, part of a development that had as big an impact on Barcelona as the 19th-century construction of the Eixample.

Fun in the sun To either side of Port Olímpic lie clean, sandy beaches, attracting both visitors and Barcelonins. The beaches stretch north from Barceloneta to the daring new Forum complex (▷ 105), which was built to host a 'cultural olympics' in 2004. Spruced up in the late 1980s, the esplanade, 8km (5 miles) long, is backed by tree-lined grassy spaces, offering cyclists, roller-bladers and strollers an escape from the city. Along with water sports and beach games you'll find freshwater showers, sunbed rental, children's playparks and all you need for a day at the beach. When the sun sets there are the *chiringuitos* (beach bars) and restaurants in the Port Olímpic to refresh and revive.

THE BASICS

🔢 K9

✉ Port Olímpic

🚇 Ciutadella – Vila Olímpica

🚌 36, 45, 59

HIGHLIGHTS

● Frank Gehry's *Lobster* sculpture
● Strolling the Passeig Marítim
● El Forum (Forum complex)
● Sandy beaches

Port Vell

- Ascent of Columbus Column
- Harbour trip on one of the *golondrinas* pleasure boats, www.lasgolondrinas.com
- 19th-century timber-clad submarine *Ictíneo*

TIPS

- On weekends there's a craft market near the Palau del Mar overlooking the Port Vell.
- Sundays are exceptionally busy, so watch your valuables.

Renovations in the early 1990s reclaimed the Old Port and reintegrated it into city life. The modern Rambla de Mar walkway extends across the water to the Maremagnum complex, at the heart of the Old Port.

Back to the sea Barcelona has often been accused of ignoring the sea on which much of its prosperity depended. In the past, the closest most tourists came to it was an ascent of the 50m (165ft) Monument a Colom (commemorating the return of Columbus from the New World in 1493) at the seaward end of the Rambla. Now, Port Vell is given over to pleasure and entertainment and most shipping activity takes place at the modern port installations to the west, although ferries to the Balearics still depart from here.

The Rambla de Mar walkway (left. The Maremagnum complex at night (top middle) and by day (right). One of the golondrine pleasure boats (bottom middle left). The Aquàrium (bottom middle right)

THE BASICS

Aquarium
www.aquariumbcn.com
🚇 G9
✉ Moll d'Espanya
☎ 93 221 74 74
🕐 Oct–end May Mon–Fri 9.30–9, Sat, Sun 9.30–9.30; Jun, Sep daily 9.30–9.30; Jul, Aug daily 9.30–11pm
🚇 Drassanes
🚌 14, 17, 36, 38, 40, 45, 57, 59, 64, 91
💰 Expensive

Monument a Colom
🚇 F/G8
✉ Plaça del Portal de la Pau
☎ 93 302 52 24
🕐 Daily 9–8.30
🚇 Barceloneta, Drassanes
🚌 14, 17, 36, 38, 40, 45, 57, 59, 64, 91
💰 Inexpensive

Peninsula The Maremagnum, a huge covered shopping and entertainment complex, at the heart of the old port, is connected to the mainland by the Rambla de Mar. This obelisk-lined walkway is usually thronged with tourists, but there are peaceful spots for a stroll. The area is particularly appealing in summer, when you want a sea breeze, and at night, when a couple of the clubs and bars are worth checking out. After a major revamp, the shopping mall in the Maremagnum is now very good, while outside you'll find the Aquàrium, which is one of the largest in Europe and requires a good couple of hours for a visit. Take a walk through the 80m-long (265ft) glass tunnel with sharks a few inches from your face. Also worthwhile is the IMAX movie house. Barcelona's *golondrinas (*swallow-boats) offer trips from the Port Vell quayside. Trips also go to Port Olímpic.

Santa Maria del Mar

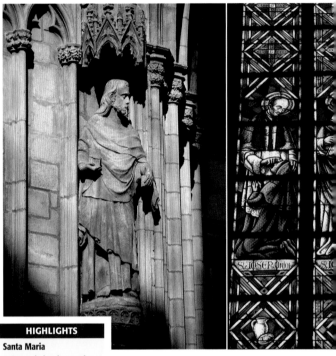

HIGHLIGHTS

Santa Maria
● Rose window in west front

In the Ribera
● Passeig del Born with central Rambla
● 19th-century glass-and-iron Born Market building
● Fosser de les Moreres plaza
● Medieval houses in Carrer Montcada

TIP

● The best time to visit is during the afternoon on a weekday, when there are fewer services.

A fortress of the faith in the old waterfront area of the Ribera, the Church of Our Lady of the Sea is one of the greatest expressions of Catalan Gothic. It was built on the proceeds of Barcelona's maritime supremacy in the Middle Ages.

The Ribera Literally 'the seaside' or 'waterfront', the Ribera was the city's hub in the 13th century, when Catalan commerce dominated the Western Mediterranean ports. Successful merchants and entrepreneurs set themselves up in fine town houses close to the busy shore, cheek by jowl with workers, dock porters and craftspeople. The street names of the Ribera still reflect the trades once practised here: Assaonadors (tanners), Espaseria (swordmaking), Argenteria (silver-smithing), Sombreres (hatters).

S·SALVADOR

People's Church Santa Maria was begun in 1329, the foundation stone commemorating the Catalan conquest of Sardinia. Sometimes referred to as the Cathedral of the Ribera, Santa Maria has always been a popular church, the focus of this once busy port district; the whole population is supposed to have toiled on its construction for 50 years. The life of the Ribera was reflected in decorative touches such as delightful depictions of dock-workers on doors and the altar. The altar is crowned by a wooden model of a 15th-century ship. Other than that, the interior of the church is almost bare; its elaborate baroque furnishings were torched during the Civil War, though the glorious stained-glass windows survived. Now the calm and symmetry created by its high vaults and by the majestic spacing of its octagonal columns can be appreciated without distraction.

THE BASICS

- ✚ H8
- ✉ Plaça de Santa Maria
- ☎ 93 310 23 90
- 🕐 Mon–Sat 9–1.30, 4.30–8, Sun 10–1, 4.30–8
- 🚇 Jaume 1
- 🚌 14, 17, 36, 39, 45, 51, 57, 59, 64
- ♿ Good (near entrance)
- 🎫 Free

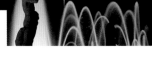

More to See

MERCAT DEL BORN

This 18th century wrought iron, covered market, closed since the 1970s, is currently being converted into a cultural hub. During the process, foundations of 18th century Barcelona were discovered, and will be on view once the project is completed.

➕ H8 ✉ Passeig del Born s/n 🚇 Jaume I

MUSEU TÈXTIL I D'INDUMENTÀRIA

www.museutextil.bcn.es

The very existence of this museum is a reminder that Barcelona rode to prosperity in the 1800s on the back of the textile industry. The collection's range extends beyond 19th-century Catalonia; there are costumes of all kinds, from the Middle Ages to more or less contemporary times—witness the inventive creations of Balenciaga. A bonus is the brace of medieval palaces housing the collection.

➕ H8 ✉ Carrer de Montcada 12 ☎ 93 319 76 83 🕐 Closed for renovations until Jun 2008 🍴 Café-restaurant 🚇 Jaume I ♿ Few ✋ Moderate

MUSEU DE XOCOLATA

www.pastisseria.com

A museum devoted to chocolate is bound to appeal to children. You'll find an overview of the history of chocolate from its New-World origins to its arrival in Europe. There are staggering chocolate creations and a tempting shop.

➕ H8 ✉ Carrer del Comerç 36 ☎ 93 268 78 78 🕐 Mon, Sat 10–7, Sun 10–3 🚇 Jaume I ✋ Moderate

PARC ZOOLÒGIC

www.zoobarcelona.com

In the Parc de la Ciutadella (▷ 66), the zoo has more than 400 species, but its reputation lies in the primates. Most of the primates are in danger of extinction, most notably the Bornean orangutans and the mangabeys, the world's smallest monkey. Other fast-disappearing animals include the Iberian wolf and various big cats. Separate children's section.

➕ J8 ☎ 93 225 67 80 🕐 Jun–end Sep daily 10–7; Mar–end May, Oct daily 10–6; Jan, Feb, Nov, Dec daily 10-5 🚇 Barceloneta, Arc de Triompf ✋ Moderate

There are more than 400 species of animals at the Parc Zoològic

La Ribera

You can experience the full range of the Born's architecture and soak up the atmosphere on this walk in the Ribera.

DISTANCE: 2km (1.2 miles)   **ALLOW:** 60 minutes

START

PLAÇA DE SANTA MARIA DEL MAR
▷ 70 ✚ H8 🚇 Jaume I

① Walk to the right of the Basilica de Santa Maria del Mar and continue onto Carrer de Santa Maria. Continue to the end to the back of the church.

② Turn left, crossing over the Placeta de Montcada and into the Carrer de Montcada. At the end of Carrer de Montcada turn right onto Carrer de la Princesa.

③ Continue to the end of Carrer de la Princesa to the Parc de la Ciutadella and the Museu de Zoologia. Turn right onto Passeig de Picasso and follow the perimeter of the park for one block.

④ Turn right onto Carrer de la Fusina and then left onto Carrer del Comerç. Here you walk around the façade of the former Mercat del Born (▷ 72).

END

PLAÇA DE SANTA MARIA DEL MAR
🚇 Jaume I

⑧ Turn right onto Carrer dels Canvis Vells. At the end of the road is the Plaça de Santa Maria del Mar.

⑦ Take Carrer del Bonaire out of the square, which farther on changes its name to Carrer del Consolat de Mar. Stop when you reach the intersection with Carrer dels Canvis Vells on your right.

⑥ Turn left onto Carrer de Palau, which brings you to the charming Plaça de les Olles, a small square with outdoor cafés and apartment blocks with pretty façades.

⑤ With your back to the market, keep left, following Carrer del Comerç to the intersection with Avinguda del Marquès de l'Argentera.

73

Shopping

ALAMACEN MARABI

www.alamacenmarabi.com
These handmade felt toys aren't cheap, but their quality and sheer charm are priceless. Kids will love the large animals and teddy bears and there are smaller items, such as finger puppets, which make unique gifts.
✚ H8 ✉ Flassaders 30bis
▣ Jaume I

ALEA MAJORAL GALERÍA DE JOYAS

www.majoral.com
Imaginative marine-inspired gold-and-silver jewellery by Balearic-born Enric Majoral is displayed at the front of this shop, while the back showroom displays pieces by some of Barcelona's up-and-coming young designers—adornment for the 21st century indeed.
✚ H8 ✉ Carrer Argentaria 66 ☎ 93 310 13 73
▣ Jaume 1

ARLEQUÍ MASCARES

www.arlequimask.com
Masks of all descriptions line the walls of this quirky shop, where the designs are inspired by influences from all over the world. Choose from a traditional Catalan mask, outrageous gilded designs or a simple Greek classic-inspired number—beautiful for decorating your home—or even wearing.
✚ H8 ✉ Carrer de Princesa 7 ☎ 93 268 27 52
▣ Jaume 1

LA BOTIFARRERÍA DE SANTA MARÍA

An array of handmade sausages, ranging from wild boar and forest mushroom to less conventional snail and sepia.
✚ H8 ✉ Carrer de Santa María 4 ☎ 93 319 91 23
▣ Jaume I

BUBO

Carles Mampel makes haute chocolate bon-bons, cakes and other goodies, which he carefully displays in this chocolate 'boutique' with the reverence of fine jewellery. Next door there is café where you can taste some before buying.
✚ H8 ✉ Carrer Caputxes 10 ☎ 93 268 72 24 ▣ Jaume I

CASA GISPERT

This establishment is an expert roaster of nuts and coffees, and sells everything from fresh-roasted hazelnuts and almonds to Iranian pistachios.

FINE DESIGN

Barcelona's design tradition and its endless array of unusual and individual shops make the hunt for gifts and accessories unusally enjoyable. Fine leather goods at reasonable prices can be found everywhere in the Eixample, and there are numerous expensive jewellery shops. In the Old Town, look for hand-painted jewellery, porcelain and wooden crafts.

✚ H8 ✉ Sombrerers 23 ☎ 93 319 75 35 ▣ Jaume I

COMO AGUA DE MAYO

This lovely shop sells a select range of stylish yet highly feminine clothing from local designers. Names to watch out for include the bold prints of Ailanto and Josep Font's quirky, retro-inspired separates. Handmade shoes and accessories also.
✚ H8 ✉ Carrer de Argenteria 43 ☎ 93 310 64 41 ▣ Jaume I

D BARCELONA

This bright, funky shop sells all sorts of designery knick-knacks for home and gifts. Local products include accessories by graphic artist Jordi Labanda and rubber toys by Cha Cha.
✚ H8 ✉ Carrer Rec 61 ☎ 93 315 07 70 ▣ Jaume I

GLAMOOR

Don't forget your prescription, because you'll find lenses and frames are less expensive here than in Britain. The funkiest frames and the hippest labels in town.
✚ H8 ✉ Carrer Calders 10 ☎ 93 310 39 92 ▣ Jaume I, Barceloneta

KITSCH

Kitsch isn't actually all that kitsch but it is certainly curious. One of its most impressive lines is the papier mâché figurines. You certainly can't miss

the particularly startling flamenco figure in the doorway, near the Santa Maria del Mar church.

🞦 H8 ✉ Placeta de Montcada 10, 08003 ☎ 93 319 57 68 Ⓜ Jaume I

LOBBY
www.lobby-bcn.com
This two-level concept store behind the Mercat del Born sells sought-after designer clothing for men and women, as well as accessories and urban knick-knacks such as agendas and key rings. Their own in-house label is surprisingly well-priced and competes with the imports in terms of style and quality.

🞦 H8 ✉ Carrer Ribera 5 ☎ 93 319 38 55 Ⓜ Jaume I

MAREMAGNUM
Best approached via the Rambla del Mar and the southwest entrance with a spectacular mirror canopy, Maremagnum, in the middle of the Old Port, contains not only fashion boutiques, but also gift shops, cafés, restaurants, bars and nightspots.

🞦 G9 ✉ Moll d'Espanya ☎ 93 225 81 00 Ⓒ Daily 10–10 Ⓜ Drassanes

MENCHÉN TOMÁS
Gorgeous frilly yet highly stylish women's wear with a distinctively French feel plus a range of delicate costume jewellery.

🞦 H8 ✉ Carrer Rec 46 ☎ 93 310 64 69 Ⓜ Jaume I

MERCAT DE SANTA CATERINA
www.mercatsantacaterina.net
Benedetta Tagliabue designed the spectacular building that has replaced Sant Pere's old market. The range, variety and quality of the produce here reflects the area's wealth—this is one of Barcelona's most desirable addresses—with everything from meat, fish and vegetables to flowers, imported groceries and luxury chocolates on offer.

🞦 H7 ✉ Passeig Lluis Companys ☎ 93 319 57 40 Ⓜ Jaume I

MINU MADHU
Come here for a superb range of shawls, scarves and elegant feminine silk jackets; scarves range from traditional Spanish fringed silk to pashminas, vibrant woollen wraps and lace and gossamer silk for evening wear.

SMALL OUTLETS
Catalonia was once known as a nation of shopkeepers and this is how most residents still shop: small outlets with personal service. Nobody seems to mind waiting for just the right cut of ham off the bone or a perfectly matching button. This sort of one-to-one contact is part of the experience for the visitor and all it takes is confidence in your communication skills.

🞦 H8 ✉ Carrer de Santa Maria 18 ☎ 93 310 27 85 Ⓜ Jaume I

OLIVE
Everything in this long, narrow shop derives from the olive, from beautifully packaged soaps and body and bath products to bottles of olive oil from Spain, Italy and all over the Mediterranean. The gift sets make a unique souvenir.

🞦 H8 ✉ Plaça de les Olles 2 ☎ 93 310 58 83 Ⓜ Jaume I

ON LAND
Urban fashion for both men and women is *de rigeur* in Josep Abril's super-hip shop, which sells his own designs and labels such as Montse Ibañes and Petit Bateau; T-shirts by Divinas Palabras are a good buy.

🞦 H8 ✉ Carrer de la Princesa 25 18 ☎ 93 310 02 11 Ⓜ Jaume I

VILA VINITECA
The number one shop for wine connoisseurs that supplies many of the city's top restaurants. The selection is so vast it is often overwhelming, but the staff is very helpful. As well as the staple tipples from La Rioja, seek out DOCs from the Priorat and Ribero del Duero, currently the most-talked about regions of wine production in Spain.

🞦 H8 ✉ Carrer Agullers 7 ☎ 93 268 32 27 Ⓜ Jaume 1

Entertainment and Nightlife

ENTERTAINMENT AND NIGHTLIFE

PORT VELL AND LA RIBERA

C.D.L.C.

www.cdlcbarcelona.com
The nightspot of FC
Barcelona, as this gig is
part-owned by Patrick
Kluivert. It has Bedouin-
style 'boudoirs' skirting the
edge of the dance floor,
two bars, and a restaurant,
right at the water's edge.
⊞ H/J9 ✉ Passeig Marítim
32 ☎ 93 224 04 70
🕐 Daily noon–3am
🚇 Ciutadella, Vila Olímpica

CLUB CATWALK

www.clubcatwalk.net
One of the better bets
amongst the handful of
nightclubs in the Vila
Olímpica area. Dark and
spacious, offering techno
downstairs and laid-back
R&B in the intimate
upstairs bars. International
DJs regularly play here,
ensuring a packed house.
⊞ J9 ✉ Carrer Ramon Trias
Fargas s/n ☎ 93 221 61 61

JAZZ ROOTS

Barcelona's love affair with
jazz goes back to before the
Civil War, when Jack Hylton's
dance band played at the
International Exhibition and
Django Reinhardt and
Stéphane Grappelli brought
the music of the Hot Club de
France to the Hot Club de
Barcelone. The tradition has
been kept alive by a continu-
al influx of American jazz
musicians including newcom-
er saxophonist Billy
McHenry, and by the city's
October Jazz Festival.

🕐 Thu–Sat midnight–5am
🚇 Cuitadella-Vila Olímpicaç

GIMLET

This cool little cocktail bar
really packs them in on
the weekends. The mixol-
ogists are the most pro-
fessional around, and
definitely know the differ-
ence between shaken
and stirred. A smooth jazz
soundtrack adds to the
ambience.
⊞ H8 ✉ Carrer Rec 24
☎ 93 310 10 27 🕐 Mon–Sat
8pm–3am 🚇 Jaume 1

LE KASBAH

On a terrace outside the
Museu d'Historia de
Catalunya, this indoor-out-
door club has special
appeal in summer when
punters lounge about on
Arabian nights style cush-
ions under the stars.
⊞ H9 ✉ Plaça de Pau Vila
s/n 93 238 07 22 🕐 Daily
10.30pm–3am 🚇 Barceloneta

MIX

www.clubmixbcn.com
This swanky bar focuses
on cocktails served by a
bevy of beautiful waitress-
es, plush surrounds and
good music. A doorman
makes sure you are wear-
ing your best threads—or
no admittance.
⊞ H8 ✉ Carrer Comerç 21
☎ 93 319 50 87 🕐 Daily
6pm–3am 🚇 Jaume 1

PALAU DE LA MÚSICA CATALANA

Domènech i Montaner's
Palace of Music has long
been Barcelona's principal

auditorium, a splendid
setting for performances
by European classical
ensembles and visiting
jazz artists. Reserve early.
⊞ H7 ✉ Carrer Sant
Francesc de Paula 2 ☎ 93
295 72 00 🚇 Urquinaona

RAZZMATAZZ

www.salarazzmatazz.com
Three nightclubs and top-
notch live music venue
(especially for indie and
electronica) in one.
⊞ K8 ✉ Carrer de Pamplona
88 ☎ 93 272 09 10 🕐 Fri
and Sat 1am–6am 🚇 Marina

EL XAMPANYET

This traditional little bar
can always be relied on
for a lively crowd, good-
value *tapas* and their
specialty, a house cava.
Seating at the small
marble tables is limited,
but the best place to sit
is at the zinc bar.
⊞ H8 ✉ Carrer Montcada
22 ☎ 93 319 70 03 🕐 Tue–
Sat 12–4pm, 6.30–11.30pm,
Sun 12–4pm 🚇 Jaume 1

PAU CASALS

The great cellist, better
known to the world as Pablo
Casals (1876–1973), was a
Catalan. In 1920, he helped
push Barcelona onto
Europe's musical map by
founding his Barcelona
Orchestra, which performed
regularly in the Palau de la
Música. In 1924–25, Igor
Stravinsky directed the
orchestra in concerts featuring his own works.

Restaurants

PRICES

Prices are approximate, based on a 3-course meal for one person.

€€€	over €50
€€	€25–€50
€	under €25

AGUA (€€)

Watch the waves while you eat at this modern, laid-back restaurant, where dishes range from modern, innovative starters to traditional Catalan fare.

➕ H/J9 ✉ Passeig Maritim de la Barceloneta 30 ☎ 93 225 12 72 🕐 Open daily 🚇 Ciutadella Vila Olímpica

BESTIAL (€€)

Arguably the best seaside terrace in Barcelona, with wood decking and parasols, offering Italian fare at reasonable prices.

➕ J8 ✉ Carrer de Ramon Trias Fargas 2–4 ☎ 93 224 04 07 🕐 Daily 🚇 Ciutadella Vila Olímpica

LA BOMBETA (€)

Most the restaurants along the Passeig de Borbón, Barceloneta's main street, are incredibly touristy, so instead steer yourself to the side of this traditional *tapas* bar. The house specialty is *bombas*; giant, fluffy croquettes topped with a spicy *brava* sauce. Other dishes such as simply grilled prawns, squid and sardines, *pá amb tomaquet* topped with *serrano*

ham or cheese and Galician-style octopus are also incredibly tasty.

➕ H9 ✉ Carrer Maquinista 3 ☎ 93 319 94 45 🕐 Closed Wed 🚇 Barceloneta

EL CANGREJO LOCO (€€)

The crowds testify to the appeal of the reasonable prices on the *menú del día* of this large Port Olímpic seafood establishment.

➕ K9 ✉ Moll de Gregal, Port Olímpic ☎ 93 221 17 48 🕐 Daily 🚇 Ciutadella Vila Olímpica

CAN RAMONET (€€)

Can Ramonet was established in 1763, and is arguably the oldest tavern in Barceloneta. The menu balances seafood, rice dishes and paellas, as well as black rice prepared with squid ink. If your appetite extends only to *tapas*, sit at one of the barrel-top tables. Should you prefer a full meal, the terrace is ideal.

➕ H9 ✉ Carrer de la

FISH FOR ALL

The seafood restaurants of Barcelona, concentrated in bayside Barceloneta, are famous. They serve *zarsuela* (a seafood stew) and *suquet de peix* (fish-and-potato soup), as well as *fideus* (a paella-style dish with noodles instead of rice). *Arròs negre* is rice cooked in the black ink of a squid.

Maquinista 17 ☎ 93 319 30 64 🕐 Closed Sun evening 🚇 Barceloneta

CAN SOLÉ (€€)

Established in the early 1900s, this elegant old eating house is tiled and decorated with photos of former famous patrons. Join the regulars to enjoy superb paellas, stickyfresh fish, lobsters and plates of sweet shrimp and prawns while watching the action in the frenetic open kitchen.

➕ H9 ✉ Carrer des Sant Carles 4 ☎ 93 221 50 12 🕐 Tue–Sat 1.30–4, 8–11, Sun 1.30–4 🚇 Barceloneta

CAVA MAR (€€)

This swanky eatery-bar has an incredible outdoor terrace facing the sea. Enjoy a bottle of cava with a plate or two, which ranges from simple *tapas* and carpaccios to lobster paella and turbot served with candied tomatoes and asparagus.

➕ H9 ✉ Carrer Vila Joisosa 54 ☎ 93 225 71 64 🕐 Daily 🚇 Barceloneta

CENTRE CULTURAL EUSKAL ETXEA (€)

For authentic regional cooking, come and join the exiles from the Basque country at their cultural hub, which serves an outstanding selection of *pintxos (tapas)* from this northern region. Expect superb seafood, tender octopus, Basque cheeses and smoked

PORT VELL AND LA RIBERA

RESTAURANTS

meats and sausages in a cozy, dark little bar.

➕ H8 ✉ Plaçeta de Montcada 1–3 ☎ 93 310 21 85 🕐 Closed Sun 🚇 Jaume I

COMERÇ 24 (€€€)

Chef Carles Abellan trained with Ferran Adrià at El Bulli, and his sophisticated restaurant follows in the master's footsteps, serving up superb new wave Catalan cooking. Sample the *menú festival* to experience what this innovative cuisine is all about—and prepare to be amazed at the tastes, textures and combinations.

➕ H8 ✉ Carrer del Comerç 24 ☎ 93 319 21 02 🕐 Closed Sun and Mon 🚇 Arc de Triomf

LITTLE ITALY (€€)

This restaurant is named after New York's Italian quarter and, although the chef is American, the food is not. The menu includes a range of pasta, meat and fish dishes, and there's a comprehensive wine list. A number of informal, comfortable rooms make up the dining space, and there is live jazz Monday to Wednesday nights.

➕ H8 ✉ Carrer del Rec 30 ☎ 93 319 79 73 🕐 Daily 🚇 Barceloneta

EL MAGATZEM DEL PORT (€€)

The grounds of Palau del Mar are home to five restaurants, all serving similar cuisine, but the small Harbour Warehouse is known for its paellas and rice dishes. The restaurant presents a creative twist on traditional recipes and the chef seeks out all his ingredients at La Boqueria market, ensuring quality and freshness.

➕ H9 ✉ Palau del Mar, Plaça de Pau Vila ☎ 93 221 06 31 🕐 Closed Mon and Sun evening 🚇 Barceloneta

LA PARADETA (€€€)

The form here is to buy a drink, inspect the mounds of mussels, clams, squid and crab and specify what you want, how you'd like it cooked and your choice of sauce. Then grab a seat at one of the refectory tables and wait till your number's called. Collect your plate and tuck in to enjoy some of the freshest and best seafood in Barcelona.

➕ H8 ✉ Carrer Comercial 7

TIPS AND TAXES

There is no fixed rule for tipping in restaurants and bars. If you have a coffee and snack leave change rounded up to the nearest euro. In all restaurants a 7 per cent VAT tax (called IVA) is added to bills, but this should not be confused with a service charge. If a full meal is served leave 5–10 per cent though in cheaper *tapas* bars, a euro or two should suffice.

☎ 93 268 19 39 🕐 Closed Tue–Thu lunch and Sun evening 🚇 Arc de Triomf

EL PASSADIS D'EN PEP (€€€)

There's no menu in this simplest of restaurants—just superb seafood, the best and freshest each day.

➕ H8 ✉ Plaça del Palau 2, La Ribera ☎ 93 310 10 21 🕐 Closed Sun, last 2 weeks of Aug 🚇 Barceloneta

SAL CAFE (€€)

Right on the waterfront, the trendy Sal Cafe serves good fish-focused dishes to stylish crowd. Book ahead for an outdoor table, though the indoor dining rooms offers views of a people-parading promenade. Hidden from street view, look its distinctive bright orange umbrellas.

➕ J9 ✉ Passeig Marítimo de la Barceloneta s/n ☎ 93 224 07 07 🕐 Closed Sun–Wed evenings 🚇 Barceloneta

SET PORTES (€€€)

Founded in 1836, the 'Seven Doors' is one of Barcelona's most famous and reliable restaurants, serving up superb paella, fish and seafood. You can book for the 1.30–2.30 and the 8–9.30 slots; otherwise be prepared to wait.

➕ H8 ✉ Passeig d'Isabel II 14, Port Vell ☎ 93 319 30 33 🕐 Daily 🚇 Barceloneta

Largely built as the city expanded in the 19th century, L'Eixample (the extension) is a grid-patterned urban area, bisected by the arrow-straight Diagonal. It's home to the city's finest *modernista* buildings.

Gràcia

Passeig de Gràcia (opposite). Relaxing in the shade (below left) and sun (below right)

This distinctive suburb is the site of the Parc Güell and a genuine Gaudí masterpiece. You'll also find peaceful squares, lively bars and a nine-day street party attracting more than 2 million each year.

Cultural village Originally a collection of tiny farms, Gràcia grew rapidly in the 19th century, becoming part of Barcelona itself in 1897. Gràcia was renowned then as a cultural and political hub, and this is reflected in some street names—Mercat de la Libertat and Plaça de la Revolució. It was also a place where music and theatre thrived and today there are exhibition areas, music societies and cultural spaces of all kinds.

Graceful Gràcia Apart from the Parc Güell (▷ 88–89), the pick of Gràcia attractions are Gaudí's exquisite Casa Vicens, one of the world's first *modernista* buildings, and Lluís Domènech i Montaner's Casa Fuster, which has been converted to a hotel. *Plaças* such as Virreina, Sol and Rius i Taulet are attractive places to pause or stop for a coffee during the day. Boasting some of the best bars and restaurants in the city, Gràcia comes into its own at night.

Summer festival The *Festa Major* has taken place annually for more than 150 years. For nine days during the second half of August, it takes over Gràcia. Each street puts up a display, with themes ranging from the Wild West to the Civil War, and the suburb is a riot of colour. You'll also find music and plays peformed outdoors on the various plaças.

THE BASICS

- ✚ G/H4
- 🍴 Many bars and cafés
- 🚇 Fontana, Gràcia, Joanic
- 🚌 22, 24, 28, 39

HIGHLIGHTS

Casa Vicens
● Elaborate exterior decoration
● Decorative wrought-iron gates

Casa Fuster
● Mix of neo-Gothic and classical styles
● Viennese-style ground floor café

Plaça Rius i Taulet
● Bell tower, designed by Antoni Rovira i Trias

Casa Milà

● Ground-floor entrance with
wall and ceiling paintings
● Rooftop
● El Pis de Pedrera: an
apartment decorated with
modernista furniture in situ
Espai Gaudí
● Audiovisual show
● Plans and models of
major buildings
● Stereofunicular model of
building structure
● Gaudí souvenir shop
(separate entrance)

TIP

● During July and August
jazz concerts are held on the
roof. Enquire about dates
and times at the ticket office.

**'Get a violin' was architect Gaudí's
response to a resident who wondered
where to install a grand piano in this
coral reef of an apartment block, which
seems designed for slithering sea crea-
tures rather than human beings.**

The grotto of the Passeig de Gràcia Anecdotes
about the Casa Milà abound: the artist Santiago
Rusinyol is supposed to have said that a snake
would be a more suitable pet here than a dog.
Lampooned for decades after its completion in
1912, this extraordinary building has been rescued
from neglect and opened to visitors. Nicknamed
La Pedrera (stone quarry), it was built for Pere
Milà Camps, a rich industrialist who afterward
complained that Gaudí's extravagance had
reduced him to penury. The steel frame that

The dramatic staircase in the Casa Milà (left). Elaborate chimney designs (middle left, bottom middle and bottom right). The façade (top right)

supports the seven-floor structure is completely concealed behind an undulating outer skin of stone bedecked with balconies whose encrustations of ironwork resemble floating fronds of seaweed. Obscured from the street, the rooftop undulates too, and is scattered with clusters of centurion-like chimneys.

One of Gaudí's greatest Gaudí originally proposed a spiral ramp that would bring automobiles to the apartment doors—an impractical idea as it turned out—but the Casa Milà nevertheless had one of the world's first underground garages. The building's beautifully brick-vaulted attics have become the Espai Gaudí, the best place to learn about Gaudí's life and work. Of particular interest are the interior photographs of some of the Gaudí buildings that are not normally open to the public.

THE BASICS

✚ G5

✉ Provença 261–265

☎ 90 240 09 73

🕐 Daily 10–8. Closed 1 and 6 Jan, 25 and 26 Dec

🚇 Diagonal

🚌 7, 16, 17, 22, 24, 28

♿ Good (but not on roof)

💷 Expensive

HIGHLIGHTS

No. 35
● Exterior sculptures
● Dome perched on columns

No. 41
● Sculpture of St. George and dragon by entrance
● Grotesque sculptures in third-floor windows
● Lamps and stained-glass panels in entrance

No. 43
● Chromatic designs on façade by Gaudí's collaborator, the artist Josep Maria Jujol

TIP

● The Casa Batlló is the only edifice open to the public. Go late afternoon for a less-crowded visit.

A century ago, the bourgeoisie of Barcelona vied with each other in commissioning ever more extravagant apartment blocks. The most extraordinary of these ornament the Block of Discord on Passeig de Gràcia.

Enlivening the Eixample In an attempt to relieve the rigidity of Cerdà's grid of streets, *modernista* architects studded the Eixample with some of the most exciting urban buildings ever seen. *Modernisme*, the uniquely Catalan contribution to late 19th-century architecture, has obvious links with art nouveau, but here it also breathes the spirit of nationalism and civic pride because Barcelona was the richest city in Spain. The Manzana de la Discòrdia juxtaposes the work of three great architects of the age.

The glittering façade (left), curved staircase (top middle) and balcony detail (bottom middle left) at Casa Batlló. The splendid St. George and Dragon sculpture on the façade of Casa Amatller (right). The wedding cake on top of Casa Lleó-Morera (bottom middle right)

No. 35 Domènech i Montaner completed the six-floor Casa Lleó-Morera in 1905. Much of this corner building was destroyed during improvements in the 1940s, but its striking *modernista* style and curved balconies have survived.

No. 41 Built in 1898 by Puig i Cadafalch, the Casa Amatller has an internal courtyard and staircase like the medieval palaces along Carrer Montcada. Outside, it is a wonderful mixture of Catalan Gothic and Flemish Renaissance, faced with bright tiles and topped by a big gable.

No. 43 The Casa Batlló reflects the hand of Antoni Gaudí, who restyled the house in 1906. It is said to represent the triumph of St. George over the dragon with its heaving roof, scaly skin of mosaic tiles, windows and tower.

THE BASICS

www.casabatllo.es

⊞ G6

✉ Passeig de Gràcia 35, 41, 43

☎ 93 216 03 06

🕐 Casa Batlló: daily 9am–8pm

Ⓜ Passeig de Gràcia

🚌 7, 16, 17, 22, 24, 28

♿ Fair

💵 Expensive

Park Güell

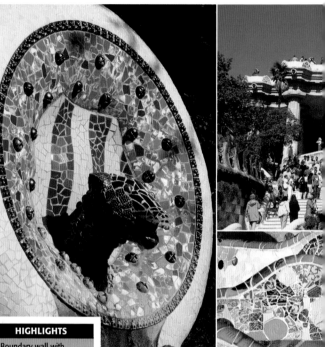

TOP 25

HIGHLIGHTS

● Boundary wall with ceramic lettering
● Ironwork of entrance gates
● Swelling forms of vaults beneath terrace
● Palm-like stonework of buttresses
● Leaning pillars of arcade
● *Modernista* furnishings in Casa Museu Gaudí

TIP

● The metro is 15 minutes' uphill walk from the park (assisted by escalators) and the only bus that stops outside is the No. 24; use the Bus Turístic if you have a ticket.

Surrealist Salvador Dalí was filled with 'unforgettable anguish' as he strolled among the uncanny architectural forms of this hilltop park, Antonio Gaudí's extraordinary piece of landscape design.

Unfulfilled intentions The rocky ridge, which has a magnificent view of Barcelona and the Mediterranean, was bought in 1895 by Gaudí's rich patron, Eusebi Güell, with the idea of developing an English-style garden city (hence the British spelling of 'park'. The project flopped; only three houses of the proposed 60 were built, and the area was taken over by the city council as a park in 1923.

Anatomy of a park The main feature is the great terrace, supported on a forest of neo-Grecian

Animal mosaic (left). The main staircase (top middle). The swirls of benches in the Gran Plaça (bottom middle). The Sala Hipóstila (right)

columns and bounded by a sinuous balustrade-cum-bench whose form was allegedly copied from the imprint left by a human body in a bed of plaster; the surface is covered by fragments of bright ceramic tiles. The strange space beneath the terrace was intended to be a market; it gapes cavernlike at the top of the steps leading from the park's main entrance.

Surreal landscape A ceramic serpent (or perhaps a dragon) slithers down the stairway toward the main entrance, which is guarded by two ginger-bread-style buildings with bulbous roofs that must be among Gaudí's oddest creations. Gaudí scattered the park with other idiosyncratic details, steps and serpentine paths. In his later years he lived in the house built by his pupil Berenguer, now the Casa Museu Gaudí.

THE BASICS

✚ H/J2
✉ Carrer d'Olot
☎ 93 219 38 11
🕐 Daily 10–8
🍽 Café
🚇 Lesseps
🚌 24, 87
♿ Few
🖐 Free

Sagrada Família

- The museum
- Seeing artisans working in situ on the new sculptures
- Elevator or stairway into tower (not for the fearful)
- Symbolic sculptures of Nativity façade

TIPS

- Start your visit by viewing the exterior from the Avenguda Gaudí.
- Cafés around the Sagrada Família are over-priced. Walk north to Avenguda Gaudí.

George Orwell thought Gaudí's great Temple of the Holy Family one of the ugliest buildings he ever saw, and wondered why the Anarchists hadn't wrecked it in the Civil War. Today it is an emblem of the city.

Devoted designer A must on every visitor's itinerary, Barcelona's most famous building is a mere fragment of what its architect intended. The ultra-pious Gaudí began work in 1883, and for the latter part of his life dedicated himself utterly to building a temple that would do penance for the materialism of the modern world. There was never any expectation that the great structure would be completed in his lifetime; his plan called for 18 high towers dominated by an even taller one, an amazing 170m (560ft) high, dedicated to Jesus

The spires on the Nativitat of La Sagrada Família (left and right) and the bridge between the towers (middle)

Christ. What he did succeed in completing was one of the towers, the major part of the east (Nativity) front, the pinnacled apse, and the crypt, where he camped out during the last months of his life before he was run down and killed by a tram. Ever since, the fate of the building has been the subject of sometimes bitter controversy.

Work in progress Many Barcelonins would have preferred the church to be left as it was at Gaudí's death, a monument to its creator. During the Civil War the Anarchists destroyed Gaudí's models and drawings though they spared the building. But enthusiasm for completion of the project was revived in the 1950s. Work has continued, though opponents believe that attempting to reproduce Gaudí's unique forms in modern materials can only lead to the creation of pastiche.

THE BASICS

www.sagradafamilia.org
+ J5
✉ Mallorca 401
☎ 93 207 30 31
🕐 Apr–end Sep daily 9–8; Oct–end Mar 9–6. Closed 25 and 26 Dec, 1 and 6 Jan
🚇 Sagrada Família
🚌 10, 19, 33, 34, 43, 44, 50, 51
♿ Moderate

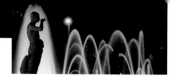

More to See

FUNDACIÓ ANTONI TÀPIES

Nowadays, Joan Miró's mantle as the Grand Old Man of Catalan art is convincingly worn by Tàpies, whose earthy creations can be seen in this magnificently converted *modernista* building by Domènech i Montaner. The building announces its purpose with Tàpies' roof-top sculpture *Cloud and Chair*, an extraordinary extrusion of wire and tubing. The foundation puts on regular shows from contemporary artists.

➕ G6 ✉ Carrer d'Aragó 255 ☎ 93 487 03 15 🕐 Tue–Sun 10–8 🚇 Passeig de Gràcia ♿ Good 🖐 Moderate

HOSPITAL DE LA SANTA CREU I SANT PAU

Disliking the monotony of the Eixample, Domènech i Montaner deliberately defied it by aligning the buildings of Barcelona's first modern hospital at 45 degrees to its grid of streets. The hospital was laid out like a self-contained village with patients housed in 48 separate pavilions; a profusion of decoration was intended to speed healing. To see inside you will need to book a tour.

➕ K4 ✉ Carrer de Sant Antoni Maria Claret 167 ☎ 90 207 66 21 🕐 Tours Mon–Thu 10.15 and 12.15 🚇 Hospital de Sant Pau 🖐 Moderate

MUSEU DEL PERFUM

www.museodelperfume.com

How appropriate that a scent museum should be set among the sleek shops and expensive boutiques of the prestigious Passeig de Gràcia. The 5,000-item collection ranges from the time of the Pharoahs to the present day.

➕ G6 ✉ Passeig de Gràcia 39 ☎ 93 216 01 21 🕐 Mon–Fri 10.30–1.30, 4.30–8, Sat 11–2. Closed hols 🚇 Passeig de Gràcia ♿ Few 🖐 Moderate

TORRE AGBAR

Designed by French architect Jean Nouvel, the striking bullet-shaped Torre Agbar is an example of the city's new breed of architecture. At night a second aluminium skin reflects blue, green and red lights, which shine through a series of slats, creating a water-like, rippling affect visible all over the Eixample area.

➕ L6 ✉ Plaça de les Glòries s/n 🚇 Glòries

Fundació Antoni Tàpies (above)
Façade of the Hospital de la Santa Creu i Sant Paul (right)

L'Eixample

A walk that combines some fine *modernista* architecture with a stroll down one of the Eixample's major shopping thoroughfares.

DISTANCE: 2km (1.2 miles) **ALLOW:** 50 minutes

START

PLAÇA JOAN CARLES I ✚ G5
🚇 Diagonal

❶ The first part of this walk assumes you have already seen the Casa Milà (▷ 84–85) and the Manzana de la Discòrdia (▷ 86–87) and leads you past some of the lesser-known *modernista* buildings of the Eixample. Walk eastward along the Diagonal which cuts through the area.

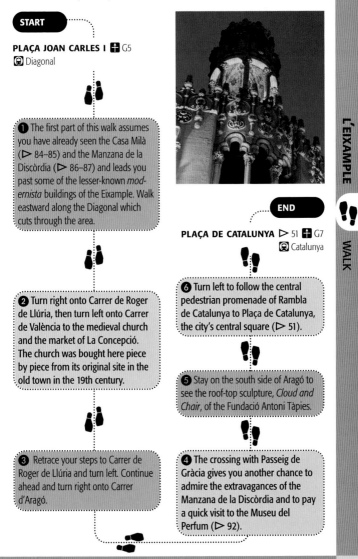

END

PLAÇA DE CATALUNYA ▷ 51 ✚ G7
🚇 Catalunya

❻ Turn left to follow the central pedestrian promenade of Rambla de Catalunya to Plaça de Catalunya, the city's central square (▷ 51).

❷ Turn right onto Carrer de Roger de Llúria, then turn left onto Carrer de València to the medieval church and the market of La Concepció. The church was bought here piece by piece from its original site in the old town in the 19th century.

❺ Stay on the south side of Aragó to see the roof-top sculpture, *Cloud and Chair*, of the Fundació Antoni Tàpies.

❸ Retrace your steps to Carrer de Roger de Llúria and turn left. Continue ahead and turn right onto Carrer d'Aragó.

❹ The crossing with Passeig de Gràcia gives you another chance to admire the extravagances of the Manzana de la Discòrdia and to pay a quick visit to the Museu del Perfum (▷ 92).

Shopping

ADOLFO DOMÍNGUEZ

One of Spain's brightest fashion stars, Domínguez's clothes for men and women manage to be mature yet achingly stylish. His 'U' range caters to a more urban look.

🏠 G6 ☒ Passeig de Gràcia 32 (and at other locations in the city hub) ☎ 93 487 41 70 🚇 Passeig de Gràcia

ALTAÏR

A profusion of books and maps on destinations worldwide, including Barcelona, Catalonia and Spain.

🏠 G6 ☒ Gran Vía de les Corts Catalans 616 ☎ 93 342 71 71 🚇 Passeig de Gràcia

ANTONIO MIRO

The first Catalan to make a name for himself in the world of fashion, Miro's men's and women's wear has remained timelessly stylish and beautifully tailored.

🏠 G6 ☒ Carrer Consell de Cent 349 ☎ 93 487 06 70 🚇 Passeig de Gràcia

ARMAND BASI

Basi is one of Spain's best-known designers and you'll find his range for both men and women at this flagship store.

🏠 G6 ☒ Passeig de Gràcia 49 ☎ 93 215 14 21 🚇 Passeig de Gràcia

BCN BOOKS

This bookshop has a good selection of classics and modern fiction from around the world in English.

🏠 H5 ☒ Roger de Llúria 118 ☎ 93 457 76 92 🚇 Diagonal

BULEVARD DELS ANTIQUARIS

Every kind of antiques dealer can be found in this complex of more than 70 shops next to the Bulevard Rosa mall.

🏠 G6 ☒ Passeig de Gràcia 55 ☎ 93 215 44 99 🚇 Passeig de Gràcia

BULEVARD ROSA

Boasts 100-plus boutiques with the best in fashion, shoes and accessories.

🏠 G6 ☒ Passeig de Gràcia 53–5 ☎ 93 215 83 31 🚇 Passeig de Gràcia

CAMPER

This Mallorca-based shoe brand, famous for mixing quirky style with comfort, have shops and outlets all over the city. But this

---

SERIOUS SHOPPING

The L'Eixample is Barcelona's serious shopping district, with the Passeig de Gràcia its jewel in the crown. This elegant avenue boasts the most expensive retail real estate in Spain, and its residents reflect this. Names such as Dolce and Gabbana and Gucci are at the northern end, while homegrown designers congregate in the south. Check out the cross-streets, too.

---

shop, a work of Spanish designer Jaime Hayon, is the most spectacular.

🏠 G6 ☒ Passeig de Gràcia 30 ☎ 93 236 45 98 🚇 Passeig de Gràcia

COLMADO QUILEZ

One of Barcelona's great food stores still retains its old mirrors and ceiling-high shelves, which are stacked with a superb variety of groceries, cheeses, hams and alcohol of every description. Saffron, anchovies and coffee are sold in beautiful packaging under Quilez' own label—as is caviar, if you really want to push the boat out.

🏠 G6 ☒ Rambla de Catalunya 63 ☎ 93 215 23 56 🚇 Passeig de Gràcia

DESIGUAL

The bright and funky streetwear from a re-madeover Spanish label is causing a stir for its quirky designs and unusual prints.

🏠 G6 ☒ Passeig de Gràcia 47 ☎ 93 304 31 64 🚇 Passeig de Gràcia

DOM

If you are into 1960s and '70s kitsch, this shop is a veritable Aladdin's cave of furniture, books and magazines, accessories and other assorted knick-knacks. Best sellers include lava lamps, chrome stools, cocktail shakers and beanbags, but smaller items such as notebooks and bags are

easy to pop into your hand luggage.
🏠 G5 ✉ Carrer Provença 249-251 ☎ 93 342 55 91 🚇 Diagonal

ELS ENCANTS FLEA MARKET

Patient searching can reveal gold among the worn clothing, broken furniture and other unwanted items. Visit around 8am for the best choice.
🏠 K6 ✉ Plaça de les Glòries ☎ 93 246 30 30 🕐 Mon, Wed, Fri, Sat 8–3 🚇 Glòries

JORDI LAMBANDA STORE

Clothing, T-shirts and stationery embellished with the stylish motifs of the city's most celebrated (and much-copied) graphic artist.
🏠 G6 ✉ Carrer Rosselló 232 ☎ 93 496 14 03 🚇 Diagonal

JOSEP FONT

Beloved by women for his feminine lines, innovative, stand-alone design and extraordinary eye for fabrics.
🏠 G5 ✉ Carrer de Provença 304 ☎ 93 487 21 10 🚇 Passeig de Gràcia

L'ILLA

One of the city's larger and better centro comerciales with loads of fashion, electronic and homeware shops, a supermarket and an extensive food court.
🏠 Off map ✉ Diagonal 555 🚌 6, 7, 30, 33, 34, 66, 67, 68

MANGO

International chain of women's fashion stores with attractive, well-made clothes in good fabrics at affordable prices.
🏠 G6 ✉ Passeig de Gràcia 65 ☎ 93 215 75 30 🚇 Passeig de Gràcia

MASSIMO DUTTI

Natty designs at more than reasonable prices in this nationwide outlet. Shirts a specialty.
🏠 G4 ✉ Via Augusta 33 ☎ 93 217 73 06 🚇 Gràcia (FGC)

SEPHORA

www.sephora.es
This French company came up with the brilliant idea of selling top-of-the-range cosmetics and scents on supermarket merchandising principles and have never looked back. Competitively priced products are ranged in order round the store, while assistants are on hand to offer samples and advice—customers are welcome to experiment.

TOMB BUS

The swanky shops along the Diagonal are hard to reach by metro. The special Tomb Bus (or shopping bus) is a people carrier that runs from outside El Corte Ingles in Plaça Catalunya north along the Passeig de Gràcia and west along the Diagonal to the L'Illa shopping mall. Hop on at any regular bus stop.

🏠 G7 ✉ El Triangle, Carrer Pelai 13–39 ☎ 93 306 39 00 🚇 Catalunya

SNÖ MITO NORDICO

For a change of pace, this shop is the only one in Barcelona that specializes in objects and clothing from Scandinavia. Fashion clothing for both sexes, as well as children.
🏠 G4 ✉ Carrer Seneca 33 ☎ 93 218 08 59 🚇 Diagonal

TOUS

This Catalan costume jewellery and leatherwear company is known all over the world. They made their mark with their iconic range of accessories featuring a teddy bear motif, but have now expanded to more sophisticated pieces.
🏠 G6 ✉ Passeig de Gràcia 75 ☎ 93 488 15 58 🚇 Diagonal

VINÇON

www.vincon.com
This large, two-floor emporium is closely tied to the city's vibrant design culture. The owner is a celebrated interior designer, and over the decades has pioneered home-grown talent, often by promoting their work in imaginative window displays. Products cover all types of homewares, plus bags, notebooks, watches and smaller items—good for gifts to take home.
🏠 G5 ✉ Passeig de Gràcia 96 ☎ 93 215 60 50 🚇 Diagonal

Ententainment and Nightlife

ANTILLA BARCELONA

The best of salsa and merengue—guaranteed good times and free dance lessons to get you going.

🚇 F6 ✉ Carrer d'Aragó 141–143 ☎ 93 451 21 51 🕐 Daily at 11pm 🚇 Hospital Clínic

BIKINI

A large club in the L'Illa shopping mall, with separate spaces for cocktails, salsa and rock.

🚇 Off map ✉ Déu I Mata 105 ☎ 93 322 00 05 🕐 Closed Mon, Tue 🚇 Les Corts

BUDA BAR

This ultra-trendy bar pulls in a super-stylish crowd, so dress up if you want to make it past the doorman. A rear restaurant serves pan-Asian cuisine, but the real attraction is the front bar and dancefloor, which pumps out cocktails to the tune of Balearic beats.

🚇 H6 ✉ Carrer Pau Claris 92 ☎ 93 318 42 52 🕐 Daily 9pm-3am 🚇 Passeig de Gràcia

CITY HALL

Three different levels blast out a range of music spanning techno to deep-house, while lounging night owls chill out on the terrace. One of downtown Barca's best places for dancing the night away.

🚇 G6 ✉ Rambla de Catalunya 2–4 ☎ 93 317 21 77 🕐 Daily until 5am 🚇 Catalunya

DRY MARTINI

This elegant, ocean liner-style cocktail bar serves the best martinis in town.

🚇 F5 ✉ Carrer d'Aribau 162–166 ☎ 93 217 50 72 🕐 Daily until 2.30am 🚇 Provença, Hospital Clínic, Diagonal

LES GENS QUE J'AIME

This basement bar has authentic Parisian *fin de siècle* touches, and is the perfect spot for an intimate cocktail on one of the velvet settees.

🚇 H5 ✉ Carrer Valencia 286 ☎ 93 215 68 79 🚇 Diagonal

LUZ DE GAS

It's worth the journey to party and listen to good music in this splendidly restored old music hall, which varies its live acts. Jazz singer Monica Green is a regular and jazz and blue bands grace the stage early in the week, giving way to rock and funk on the weekends.

🚇 F3 ✉ Carrer de Muntaner 246 ☎ 93 209 77 11 🚇 FGC Muntaner

QUIET PLEASE

Stringent new laws on noise are playing havoc with the city's nightlife. Many bars and clubs are having to close, either permanently or while they soundproof their venues, or move to less residential spots. Revellers are asked to do their bit by keeping their voices down while waiting in line or leaving a bar.

MOVIE

This lounge-club has not forgotten its former life as a cinema, so DJs (or VJs) put on audiovisual shows of classic film excerpts set to modern music. Food is served from the old cinema seats while watching the show.

🚇 H6 ✉ Carrer Roger de Llúria 50 ☎ 93 467 54 81 🕐 Closed Sun–Tues 🚇 Passeig de Gracia

OTTO ZUTZ

This club is still the place to see and be seen for Barcelona's glitterati and those aspiring to join them. Clever lighting and metal staircases and galleries set the scene.

🚇 G4 ✉ Carrer de Lincoln 15 ☎ 93 238 07 22 🕐 Wed–Sat 🚇 Gràcia

SUTTON

Plush, chic club that used to be a gathering place for the over fifties; a change of management has seen the focus put on younger, but not too young, clubbers. Dress up.

🚇 G4 ✉ Carrer Tuset 13 ☎ 93 414 42 17 🕐 Closed Sun, Mon 🚇 Diagonal

TEATRE NACIONAL DE CATALUNYA

Catalonia's official public playhouse has its own resident company. Famous Spanish and international productions are staged.

🚇 Off map ✉ Plaça de les Arts 1 ☎ 93 306 57 00 🚇 Glóries

Restaurants

PRICES

Prices are approximate, based on a 3-course meal for one person.

€€€	over €50
€€	€25–€50
€	under €25

ALKIMIA (€€€)

The stark, minimal dining room can be a little sober, but it's the food that matters here. Chef Jordi Vila's brilliant cooking has won the hearts of Barcelona's foodies.
🔢 J4/5 ✉ Carrer de la Industria 79 ☎ 93 207 61 15 🕐 Closed Sun, Sun 🚇 Sagrada Família

EL ASADOR DE BURGOS (€€€)

For a taste of the meat-heavy northern Spanish diet head for this traditional Castilian grill house, where whole suckling pigs, tender within and crackling without, and racks of lamb are roasted in the wood-fired oven. Other choices include sausages, superb ham and choice morsels of offal, with good house wine if you don't want to pay the high prices for others on the list.
🔢 H5 ✉ Carrer del Bruc 118 ☎ 93 207 31 60 🕐 Mon–Sat 1–4, 9–11 🚇 Verdaguer

BOTAFUMEIRO (€€€)

This spacious Galician restaurant on Gràcia's main street serves delicious shellfish and a selection of seafood from the Atlantic coast.
🔢 G4 ✉ Gran de Gràcia 81, Gràcia ☎ 93 218 42 30 🕐 Daily 🚇 Fontana

CACAO SAMPAKA (€)

A small chain specializing in haute cuisine chocolate, which they sell in stylish packaging and unusual tastes. There is a rear café, where the hot chocolate is on tap and sandwiches and cakes are deliciously sinful. It's great for a late breakfast, or a calorie-ridden afternoon tea after shopping.
🔢 G6 ✉ Carrer Consell de Cent 292 ☎ 93 272 08 33 🕐 Closed Sun 🚇 Passeig de Gràcia

CASA CALVET (€€€)

This beautiful, modern restaurant is housed in a Gaudí building and specializes in cutting-edge Catalan cuisine. The

SPANISH MEATS

Although pork is the mainstay of meat dishes, there is plenty of choice for carnivores, including brains, sweetbreads, trotters and other items that have vanished from other nations' tables. Beef and lamb are good, and game is excellent, including pheasant, partridge and wild boar (and don't ignore the humble rabbit). Try unusual combinations like duck with pears or meat with seafood.

service and ambience are all you would expect in a top-class establishment.
🔢 H6 ✉ Carrer de Casp 48 ☎ 93 412 40 12 🕐 Closed Sun 🚇 Urquinaona

CATA 1.81 (€€)

Tapas is given a modern, innovative twist in this cutting-edge restaurant, preferred by the city's foodies. Carefully selected wines from all over Spain complete the gastronomic experience.
🔢 F5 ✉ Carrer Valencia 181 ☎ 93 323 68 18 🕐 Dinner only; closed Sun 🚇 Passeig de Gràcia

CERVECERIA CATALANA (€)

It's generally agreed that the Cerveceria Catalana serves the best *tapas* in town, so getting a table here can often require patience (they don't take bookings). Instead grab a seat at the bar and peruse their mouthwatering array of morsels.
🔢 G5 ✉ Carrer Mallorca 236 93 216 03 68 🕐 Daily 🚇 Passeig de Gracia

CHIDO ONE (€€)

Crammed full of Mexican kitsch and tequila bottles, the authentic Mexican dishes here include mammoth *burritos*, gusty *mole* sauces, mouth-puckering ceviches and vats of fiery *salsa*.
🔢 H4 ✉ Carrer de Torrijos 30 ☎ 93 285 03 35 🕐 Mon–Fri 7pm–2am, Sat, Sun 1pm–2am 🚇 Fontana

CINC SENTITS (€€€)

Ingredients sourced from all over the world are lovingly and inspirationally combined at this cutting-edge restaurant, the 'Five Senses'. Dishes range from simple grills with a twist to slow-cooked braises with imaginative vegetable pairings. Puddings are light or rich, whichever you fancy, and the wine list is extensive.
➕ F6 ✉ Carrer d'Aribau 58 ☎ 93 323 94 91 🕐 Mon 1.30–3.30, Tue–Sat 1.30–3.30, 8.30–11 🚇 Passeig de Gràcia

HABALUC (€€)

This smart eatery serves organic, mostly vegetarian dishes to an equally smart crowd. Expect risottos and stir-fries in the evenings or a great value *menú del día* at lunchtime. Meat eaters should easily be appeased by the great burgers and carpaccios.
➕ G5 ✉ Carrer Enric Granados 41 ☎ 93 452 29 28 🕐 Closed Sun 🚇 Provença (FGC)

JAUME DE PROVENÇA (€€€)

Interesting international dishes vary a menu of Catalan specialties, all prepared with refinement by acclaimed local chef Jaume Bargués.
➕ E5 ✉ Carrer de Provença 88 ☎ 93 322 79 31 🕐 Closed Mon and Sun dinner, Aug, Christmas and Easter 🚇 Entença

JEAN LUC FIGUERAS (€€€)

This elegant restaurant at the bottom end of Gràcia, just off the Diagonal, offers superb Catalan cuisine—and the best desserts in the city.
➕ H5 ✉ Santa Teresa 10 ☎ 93 415 28 77 🕐 Closed Sun 🚇 Diagonal

MOO (€€€)

The ultra trendy Omm Hotel hosts Moo, one of the city's most talked-about restaurants. Run by the Michelin-starred Roca Brothers, the best way to taste their quirky, molecular cookery is with a tasting menu—expect to end the multi-course meal with a dessert inspired by a famous perfume.
➕ G5 ✉ Carrer Rosselló 265 ☎ 93 445 40 00 🕐 Daily 🚇 Diagonal

SPECIAL TODAY

Many local people make lunch the main meal of the day and eat relatively frugally in the evening. One reason for following their example is to benefit from the bargain represented by the *menú del día* (fixed-price menu). It is likely to consist of three or four courses plus bread and a drink, a combination that would cost considerably more if the dishes were selected individually, particularly in the evening.

NOTI (€€€)

A favorite for the city's media set, a former HQ of a newspaper has been dramtically done-over in the bold colours of the bullfight (red, fuschia and black). The food however is firmly based in Mediterranean cuisine with great steaks and a few Asian dishes rounding the menu off. Although slightly pricier than the norm, their *menú del día* is good value.
➕ H6 ✉ Carrer Roger de Llúria 35 ☎ 93 342 66 73 🕐 Closed Sun and Sat lunch 🚇 Urquinaona

L'OLIVÉ (€€)

Good service and delicious Catalan meat and seafood dishes in a traditional setting.
➕ G6 ✉ Carrer de Balmes 47 ☎ 93 452 19 90 🕐 Closed Sun evening 🚇 Universitat

LE RELAIS DE VENISE (€€)

This meat lovers' paradise serves nothing but fat, juicy steaks, perfect *pommes frites* and green salads. Fear not if the portions look small, that's only round one.
➕ G/H5 ✉ Carrer de Pau Claris 142 ☎ 93 467 21 62 🕐 Daily 🚇 Passeig de Gràcia

Around the central city, there's a clutch of sights that combine Barcelona's history with its present-day preoccupations. Pedralbes gives an insight into the medieval world and grand early-20th-century living, while Tibidabo and Nou Camp represent its modern pleasures.

Parc de
les Heures

B-20

RONDA DE DALT

RONDA DE DALT

B-20

Parc de la
Guineueta

Parc de la
Creueta
del Coll

Parc del Turó
de la Peira

Park
Güell

TUNEL DE LA ROVIRA

Parc del
Guinardó

TRAVESSERA DE DALT

GRÀCIA

RONDA DEL GUINARDÓ

Parc de
les Aigües

AVINGUDA MERIDIANA

Parc
Pegaso

SAGRADA
FAMÍLIA

AVINGUDA DIAGONAL

CARRER D'ARAGÓ

Parc
del Clot

VIA DE LES CORTS CATALANES

C-31

AVINGUDA MERIDIANA

Parc Estació
del Nord

AVINGUDA DIAGONAL

LA RIBERA

PASSEIG DE PICASSO

CARRER DE LA MARINA

Parc
de la
Ciutadella

Parc
Diagonal
Mar

RONDA LITORAL

Parc del
Poblenou

B-10

El Forum

PORT
OLÍMPIC

0   1 km

0   1 mile

Museu Monestir de Pedralbes

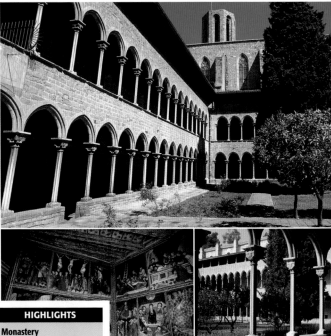

TOP 25

FARTHER AFIELD   TOP 25

HIGHLIGHTS

Monastery
● Chapel of San Miguel, with 14th-century paintings by Spanish painter and miniaturist Ferrer Bassa
● Tomb of Queen Elisenda, the monastery's founder
● Dioramas of the *Life of Christ* by Joan Mari

TIP

● Combine your trip to the museum with other sights in the area or a visit to the church next door. Open Tue–Sun 11am–2pm and 6.30–8pm (☎ 93 203 77 79). Nuns sing during the daily mass at 7pm.

Only a bus ride away from the bustle of central Barcelona stands one of Europe's best-preserved and most atmospheric medieval monasteries. It has an intriguing museum of monastic life.

Monastic museum Once a foothill village outside Barcelona, Pedralbes still exudes a rustic atmosphere, with a cobbled street leading steeply upward to the fortresslike walls of the great monastery. The nuns first came here in the 14th century and their successors still worship in the austere church. They have had a new residence since 1983, and the historic parts of the monastery have become a fascinating museum of monastic life. The building contains numerous works of art, liturgical objects and furniture that the nuns accumulated over the centuries. The core of the

The courtyard of the Monestir de Pedralbes (top left), an alcove in the wall (right), a view of the tranquil gardens from the cloisters (bottom middle) and painted panels within the monastery (bottom left)

establishment is the Gothic cloister, three floors high, with elegant columns and capitals. In the middle are palms, orange trees and cypresses; around it are the spaces that once housed community activities. The simple cells contrast with the grandeur of the refectory with its vaulted ceiling, and you'll see a pharmacy, an infirmary, the kitchens and the great cistern. The chapter house has mementos of monastic life, including the funereal urn of Sobirana de Olzet, the first abbess.

The Church of Pedralbes The nuns still worship in the Gothic church next to the monastery and the sounds of their vespers are often heard in the street outside. A popular place for locals to tie the knot, it is said that if the bride brings the nuns a dozen eggs the day before the ceremony it won't rain on her wedding day.

THE BASICS

➕ C1
✉ Baixada del Monestir 9
☎ 93 256 34 34
🕐 Tue–Sun 10–2. Closed 1 Jan, 1 May, 24 Jun, 25 Dec, Easter Sun
🚇 Reina Elisenda
🚌 22, 63, 64, 78
♿ Good
💶 Moderate, free first Sun of month (combined ticket with the Museu d'Història de la Ciutat)

Palau de Pedralbes

The mansion house and pool (left) and enjoying the sunshine in the grounds (right)

THE BASICS

➕ C2
✉ Diagonal 686
☎ 93 280 50 24
🕐 Tue–Sat 10–6, Sun 10–3. Closed 1 Jan, 1 May, 24 Jun, 25 and 26 Dec
🚇 Palau Reial
🚌 7, 33, 67, 68, 74, 75
♿ Fair
💷 Moderate; gardens free (ticket admits to both museums)

HIGHLIGHTS

● Pavellons Güell: separate entrance at Avinguda de Pedrables. Interior visits by guided tour ☎ 93 317 76 52
● Garden pools and fountains
● Forecourt statue of Queen Isabel II

Museums
● Medieval Mudejar ware
● Ceramic works by Miró and Picasso
● *Modernista* bed of 1908
● Art deco glass
● 1930–90 Industrial Design Collection

When Spanish royals opened the 1888 Expo, Barcelona had to lodge them unceremoniously in the town hall. By the time of the second Expo in 1929, the king was able to stay in this fine villa.

Preparing a palace The city fathers' solution to the lack of a palace was engineered by J. A. Güell, son of architect Gaudí's great patron. The grounds of the family's villa in Pedralbes already had a Gaudí gatehouse; in the 1920s wings were added to the villa and the gardens were lavishly land-scaped—all in time for King Alfonso's first visit in 1926. The ill-fated monarch came again, in 1929, to participate in the grand opening of the Expo, but with the proclamation of the Spanish Republic in 1931, the palace became city property. During Franco's rule, it was visited by the dictator, who loved the finer things in life. The Generalissimo left no trace of his presence, but a pair of grand thrones grace the otherwise empty Throne Room.

Ceramics and decorative arts The palace was opened to the public in 1960 and is now the splendid setting for two fascinating museums. The superlative collection of the Museu de Ceràmica explores the substantial Spanish contribution to the craft since the 12th century. The displays of the Museu de les Arts Decoratives make a won-derful introduction to the evolution of the decora-tive arts from the early Middle Ages onward. The 20th-century exhibits, encompassing the eras of *Modernisme* to Minimalism, are ample evidence of Barcelona's claims to pre-eminence in design.

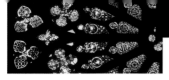

More to See

COSMOCAIXA

www.cosmocaixa.es

Housed in a splendid *modernista* building at the foot of the Tibidabo heights, this Museum of Science is the finest of its kind in Spain. Many exhibits and displays encourage participation, and it is loved by children, who have exclusive use of some of the facilities.

✚ G1 ⌧ Carrer de Teodor Roviralta 55 ☎ 93 212 60 50 🕐 Tue–Sun 10–8 🍴 Café 🚇 Tibidabo, then Tramvia Blau 🏛 Good 💶 Moderate

EL FORUM

In 2004 the city held a six-month-long 'cultural olympics' in this purpose-built site. The success of the event was debatable, but its legacy, the massive Forum complex, is an asset to Barcelona's outdoor public spaces. It's now mainly used for large-scale music events, but at other times you are free to wander. The stunning cobalt blue Forum building, designed by Swiss architects Jacques Herzog and Pierre de Mueron, sits at the entrance and is surrounded by highly stylized concrete parks and plazas that lead to a water-side marina, baths and a huge solar panel jutting out over the sea.

✚ Off Map ⌧ Rambla Prim 1 🚇 El Maresme/Fòrum

NOU CAMP

www.fcbarcelona.com

The suppression of Catalan self-respect under the Franco regime made FC Barcelona a potent symbol of identity. The passion 'Barça' attracted then, particularly when pitted against rival Real Madrid, has not diminished despite a more enlightened political climate. The 98,000-seat Nou Camp stadium is the home of the club and a great shrine of world soccer. If you want to go to a match, reserve early; most seats will be taken by the club's 125,000-plus members. The museum under the terraces has trophies and replays of magic moments. Stadium tours available.

Museo del Futbol Club Barcelona

✚ B3 ⌧ Arístides Maillol ☎ 93 496 36 00 🕐 Mon–Sat 10–8, Sun, hols 10–2 🚇 Collblanc, Maria Cristina 🏛 Good 💶 Moderate

Nou Camp stadium, home of FC Barcelona

PARC D'ATRACCIONS DE TIBIDABO

Built on several levels of the mountaintop, high-tech attractions sit alongside traditional fairground rides—some features, like the red monoplane (1922) and the Haunted Castle (1955), have entertained for years. Cota 500 is a mini version of the park with its attractions especially aimed at younger children.

➕ Off map ✉ Plaça del Tibidabo ☎ 93 211 79 42 🕐 Jul–end Aug Wed–Sat noon–11; times can vary other months, check website. Cota 500: daily 11–5 🚟 FGC Tibidabo then Tramvia Blau and funicular to park 💲 Expensive

PARC DE COLLSEROLA

www.parcdecollserola.net
An 8,000ha (19,760-acre) rural park north of the city. Many bring their bikes and ride along the Carretera de les Aigües, a route that skirts along the bases of Tibidabo and offers great views. There are lots of well-posted walking tracks where you may spot some of the local wildlife, which includes the famous *jabali* (wild boar). The park contains the Museu-Casa Verdaguer, former home of Catalonia's most revered poet. The park's information centre can help you out with maps and advice.

➕ Off map ✉ Information centre: Carretera de Vallvidrera a Sant Cugat ☎ Information centre 93 280 35 52; museum 93 204 78 05 🕐 Information centre daily 9.30–3; museum Sat, Sun and hols 10–2 🍴 Bar/restaurant 🚟 Baixador de Vallvidrera (FGC) then short walk 💲 Museum moderate

TORRE DE COLLSEROLA

This spiky, futuristic landmark high on the hills of Collserola was built as a communications tower for the 1992 Olympic Games. It's the highest point in the city, and visitors can ascend it via an elevator to the mirador, which affords breathtaking views.

➕ Off Map ✉ Carretera de Vallvidrera al Tibidabo s/n ☎ 93 406 93 54 🕐 Jul, Aug daily 11–8 (Mon–Fri closed for lunch); Apr–end Jun, Sep Wed–Sun 11–7; Oct–end Mar 11–6 🚟 Peu de Funicular (FGC) then funicular and bus 11 💲 Moderate

All the fun of the fair at Tibidabo (left)

A view from Tibidabo toward the Torre de Collserola (below)

There's plenty of choice for places to stay in Barcelona, whatever your budget. It's worth checking out the internet before leaving home to catch some seasonal deals.

Introduction

All accommodation in Catalonia is officially regulated by the Generalitat, the regional government, and is broken down into two categories.

Hotels are denoted by (H) and rated on a scale of one to five stars. All rooms must have a private bathroom to qualify as a hotel, and the number of stars is determined by the amenities each hotel provides. Simpler hotels rarely have restaurants or provide breakfast.

Hostals (HS) sometimes classify themselves as *fondes*, *pensións* or *residències.* They're rated on a scale of one to three stars and are normally less expensive than hotels. Many have been renovated over the past 15 years or so and will have a number of rooms with bathrooms. *Hostals* tend to be family-run, very few have restaurants and many do not serve breakfast.

In the past five years Barcelona has seen an explosion of smart urban hotels. Facilities such as rooftop pools, stylish lobbies and designer features are becoming more and more common, and can often be had for the price of a regular three star.

Despite this plethora of new accommodation, finding a room in Barcelona can be difficult, especially during major trade events, so it pays to book as far ahead as you can to secure something central. If you haven't reserved a room in advance, the tourist offices in the Plaça de Catalunya and the Plaça de Sant Jaume have hotel reservation desks where you will usually be able to find something. They charge a deposit against the cost of the room. Once at the hotel ask to see the room before you make up your mind.

WHERE TO STAY

If you want to be in heart of the action, reserve accommodation around the Ramblas or in the Barri Gòtic, where there's a huge choice, including budget options. The quieter Eixample, too, is well endowed with hotels, and is generally safer than downtown. Nicest of all are either the classy Ribera, or Gracia, with its laid-back, intimate atmosphere.

Budget Hotels

PRICES

Expect to pay between €50 and €80 for a budget hotel

CHIC & BASIC TALLERS

www.chicandbasic.com
The name says it all for this boutique hostal. Rooms are a bit small, but decked out in minimalist decor and extras such as flat-screen TVs and iPod docks up the ante of most hotels in this price range.
➕ G7 ✉ Carrer Tallers 82
☎ 93 302 51 83
🚇 Universitat

ESPAÑA

www.hotelespanya.com
The glory days of the España may be over, but the public rooms of this turn-of-the-20th-century *modernista* edifice off the Rambla, decorated by some of the finest artists of the time, still stand out. The 80 guest rooms are more functional than *modernista*, but are well equipped.
➕ F8 ✉ Carrer de Sant Pau
9 ☎ 93 318 17 58; fax 93 317 11 34 🚇 Liceu

GÒTICO

www.hotelgotico.com
A well-established and comfortable choice in the middle of the Barri Gòtic. Upper end of the range, with 80 rooms.
➕ G8 ✉ Carrer de Jaume I
14 ☎ 93 315 22 11; fax 93 315 31 13 🚇 Jaume I

HOSTAL GAT RAVAL

www.gataccommodation.com
This second-floor *hostal* provides everything the modern urban visitor needs, from internet access to abstract art impressions on the walls. There is a second branch —called Gat Xino—nearby. In both, most of the bathrooms are communal.
➕ F7 ✉ Carrer de Joaquín Costa 44 ☎ 93 481 66 70; fax 93 342 66 97 🚇 Universitat

HOSTAL GIRONA

www.hostalgirona.com
The reception area, with its antique furniture and Persian rugs, gives a fore-taste of the quality of this superb *hostal*. Rooms are bright and simple, with big windows and tiled floors; some have private bathrooms, and many have balconies overlook-ing Carrer Girona or the inner courtyard.
➕ H7 ✉ Carrer de Girona

SELF-CATERING

Barcelona has hundreds of self-catering holiday apart-ments available for short-term rent. Unless you are in Barcelona already, the best place to reserve self-catering accommodation is on the internet. Reputable agencies include www.oh-barcelona. com and www.selfcatering-holidays.com. Check out the location from an independ-ent source such as www.tmb.net and ask about extra costs such as cleaning.

24 ☎ 93 265 02 59; fax 93 265 85 32 🚇 Urquinaona

HOSTAL LAUSANNE

www.hostallausanne.es
Take the elevator to reach this 17 room, first-floor *hostal* run by a friendly family. The spacious, high-ceilinged rooms are bright and clean, and some have balconies.
➕ G7 ✉ Avinguda del Portal de l'Angel 24 ☎ 93 302 11 39 🚇 Catalunya

HOSTAL ORLEANS

www.hostalorleans.com
Between Barceloneta's beach and the trendy El Born district, you couldn't do much better for accommodation on a budget. Most rooms have been refurbished and are comfortable with en suites. Some look out onto a busy thoroughfare, so if noise is an issue ask for an interior room.
➕ H8 ✉ Avinguda Marquès de Argentera 13 ☎ 93 319 73 82; fax 93 319 2219 🚇 Barceloneta

HOSTAL D'UXELLES

www.hotelduxelles.com
Away from the major sites, this charming hostal has 14 rooms in a 19th-century building. Rooms are decked out with pret-ty fabrics and rustic antiques, some have small terraces and most have balconies.
➕ H6 ✉ Gran Via de les Corts Catalanes 688 ☎ 93 265 25 60; fax 93 232 85 67 🚇 Tetuan

WHERE TO STAY BUDGET HOTELS

109

Mid-Range Hotels

PRICES

Expect to pay between €80 and €150 for a mid-range hotel

BANYS ORIENTALS

www.hotelbanysoriental.com
Situated on one of the Born's most bustling streets, this friendly little *hostal* lives up to the area's style credentials without skimping on the service. A gem.
✚ H8 ✉ Carr de Argentería 37 ☎ 93 268 84 60; fax 93 268 84 61 🚇 Jaume 1

CONTINENTAL PALACETE

www.hotelpalacete.com
Enjoy the period ambience at this refurbished 19th-century palace, where you can dine under the glittering chandelier in sumptuous white-and-gold surroundings. Traditional elegance is combined with modern practicality in the 19 rooms, some that overlook Rambla de Catalunya. Room and laundry service, bar and internet access are available, plus a 24-hour light buffet.
✚ G6 ✉ Rambla de Catalunya 30 ☎ 93 487 17 00; fax 93 445 00 50 🚇 Passeig de Gràcia

GAUDÍ

www.hotelgaudi.es
No idle use of the great architect's name, this 73-room, modern hotel has an enviable location opposite the Palau Güell.
✚ G8 ✉ Carrer Nou de la Rambla 12 ☎ 93 317 90 32; fax 93 412 26 36 🚇 Liceu

HOTEL 54

www.hotel54barceloneta.com
The ultra-urban Hotel 54 is the only accommodation in Barceloneta, so if staying a stone's throw from the beach in stylish surrounds sounds appealing then look no further. Rooms are small, but with all the designer trappings and fabulous views of the port from curtain glass windows. The rooftop bar and terrace is a great place to chill out.
✚ H9 ✉ Passeig de Joan de Borbo 54 ☎ 93 225 00 54; fax 93 225 00 80 🚇 Barceloneta

HOTEL BALMES

www.derbyhotels.com
A small outdoor pool in a pretty rear garden sets this great-value, three-star hotel apart from the rest in its category, and can prove a god send in the hot summer months. Conveniently close to the shopping hub of Passeig

RESERVING ACCOMMODATION

Barcelona is a great magnet for business visitors, and reserving early is a must if you are to have much choice in where to stay. The past decade's building boom boosted the number of luxury hotels, but also swept away some of the more modest accommodation.

de Gràcia, the Balmes' rooms, while not overly spacious, are stylish and comfortable and an impressive collection of Egyptian art is scattered throughout the marble-lined lobby.
✚ G5 ✉ Carrer Mallorca 216 ☎ 93 451 19 14; fax 93 451 00 49 🚇 Diagonal

HOTEL CONSTANZA

www.hotelconstanza.com
Great value for money, this elegant, Japanese-inspired boutique hotel is brilliantly situated for shopping and sights, plus it goes overboard on luxury complimentary toiletries.
✚ H6 ✉ Carrer del Bruc 33 ☎ 93 317 40 24; fax 93 217 40 24 🚇 Urquinaona

HOTEL JARDÍ

www.hoteljardi-barcelona.com
If you want to stay in the heart of the action, you couldn't do better than the Jardí, with its superb position overlooking two of the Barri Gòtic's most beguiling squares. Rooms are big, clean and functional and all have private bathrooms; it's worth paying the extra for one with a balcony overlooking the front.
✚ G7 ✉ Plaça de Sant Josep Oriol/Plaça del Pí ☎ 93 301 59 00; fax 93 342 57 33 🚇 Liceu

HOTEL PULITZER

www.hotelpulitzer.es
The Pullitzer stands just behind the Plaça Catalunya, providing stylish hotel comfort in the city's

main hub. The rooms and public areas contain an impressive collection of antiques and abstract art, and the Japanese-style bathrooms and rooftop terrace are a real draw.
⊕ G7 ✉ Carrer Bergara 8 ☎ 93 481 67 67; fax 93 481 64 64 🚇 Catalunya

HOTEL SANT ANGELO
www.nh-hotels.com
A smallish hotel right beside the Joan Miró park, with good facilities, 48 comfortable rooms, and a relaxed lounge area, which opens onto an inner courtyard.
⊕ E6 ✉ Carrer del Consell de Cent 74 ☎ 93 423 46 47; fax 93 423 88 40 🚇 Rocafort

HOTEL SANT AUGUSTÍ
www.hotelsa.com
This old monastery building on a tree-shaded Raval square was converted to a hotel in 1840, making it the oldest in Barcelona. It's kept up with the times and its handsome, high-ceilinged rooms are now well-equipped and comfortable; two are suitable for disabled guests. The greenery-filled, elegant marble lobby gives access to a relaxing bar and hotel restaurant.
⊕ G7 ✉ Plaça de Sant Agustí 3 ☎ 93 318 16 58; fax 93 317 29 28 🚇 Liceu

HOTEL SOHO
www.nnhotels.es
This 54-room hotel wears its 'designer' stripes loud and proud, but unlike other in its genre, the mod-con trappings actually enhance your stay rather than merely decorate it. Clever lighting in the rooms can be manipulated to suit your mood, and furniture can be easily moved around to suit your needs. Ask for a rear room, which are not only quieter but have a spacious terrace overlooking a courtyard.
⊕ F6 ✉ Gran Via de les Corts Catalanes 543-545 ☎ 93 552 96 10; fax 93 552 96 11 🚇 Urgell

HUSA ORIENTE
www.husa.es
At the somewhat seedy lower end of the Rambla, the mid-19th-century Oriente has long since ceased to be *the* place to stay in Barcelona, but its ornate public spaces and only slightly less alluring 142 rooms continue to attract customers who like lodgings with some character. Previous guests here include Hans Christian Andersen and Errol Flynn.
⊕ G8 ✉ La Rambla 45 ☎ 93 302 25 58; fax 93 412 38 19 🚇 Liceu, Drassanes

FIRST-TIME VISITORS
The concentration of hotels around the Rambla and within easy walking distance of Plaça de Catalunya makes this area of the city an obvious choice for first-time visitors.

MARKET HOTEL
www.markethotel.com.es
Above a smart restaurant of the same name and near the Sant Antoni food market, this hotel offers stylish comfort that is normally associated with much more expensive hotels. Rooms boast hardwood floors, oriental Zen-inspired furniture, quality linen and abstract art. The two self-catering apartments with terraces are unbeatable value. With only 17 rooms, you will need to book ahead.
⊕ E7 ✉ Carrer Sant Antoni Abad 10 ☎ 93 325 12 05 🚇 Sant Antoni

SUIZO
www.hotelsuizo.com
The welcoming Suizo is a good choice in the Barri Gòtic, with its 60 comfortable rooms. There's a coffee shop, snack bar and lounge.
⊕ G8 ✉ Plaça de l'Angel 12 ☎ 93 310 61 08; fax 93 315 04 61 🚇 Jaume I

TURÍN
www.hotelturin.com
This three-star hotel, in a peaceful street in the heart of the city, was renovated in 2007. The 59 comfortable rooms are stylish and functional. All have balconies, and there's a restaurant, conference rooms, a cafeteria and parking, and a roof terrace overlooking the Raval area.
⊕ G7 ✉ Carrer del Pintor Fortuny 9 ☎ 93 302 48 12; fax 93 302 10 05 🚇 Catalunya

Luxury Hotels

PRICES

Expect to pay between €150 and €350 for a luxury hotel

ARTS BARCELONA

www.ritzcarlton.com
482 up-to-the-minute luxury rooms in two 44-floor towers, Spain's tallest buildings, overlooking the Port Olímpic.
🞣 J9 ✉ Carrer de la Marina 19–21 ☎ 93 221 10 00; fax 93 221 10 70
🚇 Ciutadella/Vila Olímpica

CASA FUSTER

www.hotelescenter.es
Designed in 1911, this magnificent building has undergone a superb restoration, which unites sleek modern design with the glory of the past. Opulent rooms retain their period features while offering cutting-edge technology and superb comfort. The ground-floor Café Vienés is a tribute to the past, while the roof terrace, with its gym, pool and bar and sweeping views, looks firmly forwards to 21st-century living.
🞣 G5 ✉ Passeig de Gràcia 132 ☎ 93 255 30 00; fax 93 255 30 02 🚇 Diagonal

CLARIS

www.derbyhotels.es
This late-19th-century town house, now a hotel of the greatest refinement, has restaurants, a fitness room, Japanese garden, rooftop terrace

with pool and Egyptian antiquities are scattered throughout. 124 rooms.
🞣 H6 ✉ Carrer de Pau Claris 150 ☎ 93 487 62 62; fax 93 215 79 70 🚇 Passeig de Gràcia

COLÓN

www.hotelcolon.es
An enviable location opposite the cathedral makes the Colón special. From the 147 rooms, specify one up front, with a view of the cathedral, although the bells are noisy.
🞣 G7 ✉ Avinguda de la Catedral 7 ☎ 93 301 14 04; fax 93 317 29 15 🚇 Jaume I

GRAN HOTEL LA FLORIDA

www.hotellaflorida.com
A good 20 minutes out of town, La Florida oozes class, from its designer suites, outdoor lap pool and stunning city views.
🞣 Off map ✉ Ctra. Vallvidrera al Tibidabo 83–93 ☎ 92 259 30 00; fax 93 259

SLEEPLESS CITY

Beware of noise. Barcelona is not a quiet city, and many of its citizens never seem to go to bed. A room on the Rambla may have a wonderful view, but without super-efficient double-glazing, undisturbed slumber cannot be guaranteed.
Accommodation overlooking an unglamorous nearby skylight may be less picturesque, but could possibly prove a wiser choice.

30 01 🚐 Hotel shuttle service to central Barcelona

HOTEL 1898

www.nnhoteles.es
One of the city's most exciting new hotels. An art deco theme prevails throughout, with potted palms, patterned floors and ship's-cabin style in the 169 rooms. Spa and rooftop pool; it's the only luxury option right on Las Ramblas.
🞣 G7 ✉ Las Ramblas 109 ☎ 93 552 95 52; fax 93 552 95 50 🚇 Catalunya

HOTEL DUQUESA DE CARDONA

www.hduquesadecardona.com
A romantic hotel in a stunning spot occupying a restored 16th-century building, which has been fitted with natural materials that focus on its air of understated luxury. Rooftop terrace with wide views, swimming pool and sunbathing area, and an elegant restaurant serving modern Catalan food.
🞣 G8 ✉ Passeig de Colom 12 ☎ 93 268 90 90; fax 93 268 29 31 🚇 Drassanes

HOTEL NERI

www.hotelneri.com
A handsome 18th palace deep in the Gothic quarter stunningly made over into a luxurious boutique hotel. Expect sumptuous, orientalist interiors combined with mod cons and smooth comfort.
🞣 G7 ✉ Carrer Sant Sever 5 ☎ 93 304 06 55; fax 93 304 03 37 🚇 Jaume 1

Use this section to familiarize yourself with travel to and within Barcelona. The Essential Facts will give you insider knowledge of the city. You'll also find a few basic language tips.

Planning Ahead

When to Go

Barcelona has no off-season—there is always something to see and do. However, May to June and mid-September to mid-November are ideal visiting times, with perfect temperatures and bearable crowds. Summer can be very hot, and you'll have to contend with huge crowds.

TIME

Spain is 6 hours ahead of New York City, 9 hours ahead of Los Angeles, and 1 hour ahead of the UK.

AVERAGE DAILY MAXIMUM TEMPERATURES											
JAN	FEB	MAR	APR	MAY	JUN	JUL	AUG	SEP	OCT	NOV	DEC
57°F	59°F	63°F	66°F	72°F	77°F	84°F	84°F	81°F	73°F	64°F	59°F
14°C	15°C	17°C	19°C	22°C	25°C	29°C	29°C	27°C	23°C	18°C	15°C

Spring (March to May) is a good time to visit; pleasantly warm, though it can be cloudy.
Summer (June to September) is the hottest season with very high temperatures in July and August.
Autumn (October to November) is normally Barcelona's wettest season, with heavy rain and thunderstorms as summer heat abates.
Winter (December to February) brings rain up to Christmas, followed by cooler, drier weather, though temperatures are rarely much below 10°C (50°F).

WHAT'S ON

January *Three Kings* (6 Jan): The kings arrive by boat and shower children with sweets.

February/March *Carnival*: Boisterous pre-Lenten celebrations include a major costumed procession and the symbolic burial of a sardine. Sitges *Carnival* is particularly festive.

Easter Celebrated in style in the outer districts with a southern Spanish population.

April *St. Jordi (St. George's Day*, 23 Apr): The festival of Catalonia's patron saint is marked by lovers' gifts:

roses for the woman, a book for the man. There are open-air book fairs and impressive floral displays.

June/July *Midsummer Sant Joan* (23–24 Jun): An excuse for mass partying and spectacular fireworks on the beaches.
Festival del Grec (Jun–Aug): A festival of music, plays and dance.

August *Festa Major de Gràcia*: Ten days of street celebrations in the city's most vibrant suburb, village-like Gràcia.

September *Diada de Catalunya* (11 Sep): Flags

wave on the Catalan National Day, and political demonstrations are likely.
Festas de la Mercé (19–25 Sep): The week-long festival celebrating the city's patron saint, Our Lady of Mercy, is Barcelona's biggest. Music, plays, flamenco dancing, parades, fireworks and spectacles featuring giants, dragons and *castellers* (human towers) all occur.

December *The Christmas Season*: Preparations include a grand crib in Plaça de Sant Jaume (▷ 48) and a market in front of the cathedral.

Useful Websites

www.barcelonaturisme.com
Barcelona's official tourist website has a wealth of information covering every aspect of the city. In English, and regularly updated, it's the obvious place to research your trip. One word of warning—the site can be slow to download.

www.spain.info
The main Spanish tourist board site is loaded with details about both Barcelona and its local environs.

www.barcelona-metropolitan.com
The city's premier English-language magazine gives the low-down on what's on and what's new in the bar, restaurant and nightclub scene, as well as inspiration for days out of town and a handy classified section for apartments and jobs.

www.barcelonahotels.es
Run by Barcelona's hotelier association, this site has a good choice of mid-range, mid-price hotels with online booking.

www.bcn.es
This site, in English, is run by Barcelona's city council and is primarily aimed at locals. There is an excellent tourism section, with details of opening times, exhibitions and more.

www.tmb.net
All you need to know about fares, routes and the timetables of Barcelona's bus and metro systems.

www.fcbarcelona.com
Even if you're not a football fan, this official site gives an insight into the passions the team evokes.

www.lecool.com
A carefully selected roundup of hip cultural and music events for the coming week.

PRIME TRAVEL SITES

www.fodors.com
A complete travel-planning site. You can research prices and weather; book air tickets, cars and rooms; ask questions (and get answers) from fellow travellers; and find links to other sites.

www.renfe.es/ingles
The official site of Spanish National Railways.

www.wunderground.com
Good weather forecasting, updated three times daily.

INTERNET CAFÉS

Barcelona is one of the easiest European city's to go online. More and more hotels are offering Wi-Fi options as do the ubiquitous Starbucks cafés. *Locutorios* are cheap call venues, with phone booths installed that let you call home at a cheaper rate than either the hotels or public phone booths. A huge percentage of these also have internet facilities. The pioneer internet café in Barcelona is easyEverything, which varies its rates according to demand. It has two giant locations at
✉ Ramblas 31 and Ronda Universitat 35
☎ 93 318 24 35
🕐 Daily 8am–2.30am

Getting There

INSURANCE

US citizens should check their insurance coverage and buy a supplementary policy as needed. EU nationals receive medical treatment on production of the European emergency health card (EHIC), an electronic card that replaced the old E–111 in 2005. You should obtain this before leaving home. Full health and travel insurance is still advised. In case of emergency go to the casualty department of any of the major hospitals; Clínic (Villaroel 170, tel 93 227 54 00, metro Hospital Clínic) and Perecamps (Avda Drassanes 13–15, tel 93 441 06 00, metro Drassanes) are the two most central.

BARCELONA AIRPORT

There are currently three terminals at El Prat; Terminal A handles most foreign airline departures and arrivals including intercontinental flights; Terminal B is dedicated to Spanish airline departures including Iberia and the One World and Star Alliance groups, which include British Aiways. Terminal C operates other domestic flights. All have cash machines, and terminals A and B have tourist information desks, currency exchanges and a full range of shops and other facilities.

AIRPORTS

Barcelona's modernized airport is at El Prat de Llobregat, 11km (7 miles) from the city. There are currently 3 terminals (see panel below) with a fourth in construction. Barcelona is served by 90 international airlines and has direct flights to more than 80 international destinations.

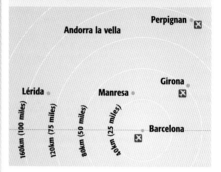

FROM BARCELONA AIRPORT (EL PRAT)

Barcelona's airport (☎ 902 40 47 04; www.aena.es) is well served by city links. The convenient Aerobus service connects both terminals with Plaça de Catalunya via Plaça d'Espanya and Gran Via de les Corts Catalanes (and Sants station for travel to the airport). The service operates every 8 minutes in both directions, 6am–1am. The journey takes around 30–40 minutes and costs €3.70.

Trains (line 10) link the airport with Sants and Estació de França. They run every 30 minutes, from 5.20am to 10.42pm, and cost around €2.50 one-way. The journey time is 33 minutes. Taxis are available outside the airport terminals; the journey takes about 20–30 minutes, depending on traffic, and costs €18–€22.

ARRIVING BY TRAIN

Barcelona is connected to all major cities within Spain and a number of destinations in Europe, namely Paris, Geneva, Zürich and Milan. These trains arrive and depart at Sants Estació, the city's main station, which also has regular bus and metro services to central

Barcelona and elsewhere. A few regional trains leave from the stations Estació de França in the old town (predominantly southbound) and from Passeig de Gràcia in the new town (mainly northbound).

ARRIVING BY BUS
Direct bus services operate from several European countries. The bus station is Estació d'Autobus Barcelona Nord, next to Arc de Triomf rail and metro station ☎ 902 26 06 06; www.barcelonanord.com.

ARRIVING BY CAR
Barcelona is connected by the AP7 toll *autopista* to the French frontier and motorway network at La Jonquera (144km/90 miles northeast). Toulouse is 368km (245 miles) north via N152, the French frontier at Puigcerdà and RN20. Motorway access to the rest of Spain is via *autopista* AP2 and AP7. However, driving is not recommended in Barcelona itself; traffic is heavy and can be intimidating, most of the city streets are part of what can be a bewildering one-way system, and parking is at a premium, with virtually no on-street parking for visitors in the downtown area. If you are driving, you could leave your car in one of the long-term airport parking areas.

ARRIVING BY SEA
Car ferry services from Britain to Spain are operated by Brittany Ferries (☎ 0870 366 53 33, Plymouth–Santander) and by P&O European Ferries (☎ 0870 242 4999, Portsmouth–Bilbao).
Ferries and cruise ships arrive at Barcelona's Port Terminal at the southern end of Las Ramblas. Ferries connect Rome and Genova in Italy and the Balearic Islands of Ibiza, Mallorca and Menorca. For the latter, the largest operator is Trasmediterranea ☎ 902 45 46 45; www.trasmediterranea.es

ENTRY REQUIREMENTS
In June 2007, the Spanish government introduced the API (Advanced Passenger Information) rule. It means all travellers need to provide the airline with the details on the photo page of their passport before departure. Many carriers have introduced a facility on their website that lets you do this online.

BUDGET AIRLINES
The explosion of inexpensive flights offered by budget airlines has made Barcelona a feasible destination for European residents looking for a short break, with easyJet flying direct to El Prat from the UK. It's worth noting that Ryanair flies into Girona, an inland town approximately one hour north of Barcelona. From here, the best method of transfer into Barcelona is the Barcelona Bus (☎ 972 18 67 08), which is timed to coincide with Ryanair flights and leaves from outside the terminal building. The journey time to the main Barcelona bus station (Estacio d'Autobus Barcelona Nord) is 1 hour and 10 minutes. Fares are €12 one-way, €21 return. Alternatively, you can take a taxi into Girona and take a train to Barcelona. These leave hourly 6.55–8.30, with a journey time of 1 hour 30 minutes for Sants station.

Getting Around

MAPS

If you want additional maps, the tourist offices provide a fairly comprehensive free street map and also sell more detailed ones at a cost of €1.20. Metro maps (ask for *una guia del metro*) are available at all metro stations, and you can pick up bus maps, which help you to make full use of the integrated TMB, city transport authority, at their main information office at metro Universitat.

VISITORS WITH DISABILITIES

Barcelona's public transport system has improved greatly for visitors with disabilities. All buses have ramps for wheelchair access and many Metro stations are being adapted with elevators. For information see www.tmb.net or look for the disabled symbol on the Metro maps. The Taxi Amic service (☎ 93 420 80 88) has wheelchair-adapted taxis; call well in advance to book. New buildings and museums have excellent facilities for visitors with disabilities, though some older attractions have yet to be converted. Check out www.accessiblebarcelona.com for lots of information on the city's wheelchair-enabled facilities and organized tours.

Although Barcelona is a walker's city *par excellence*, at some point you will need to use the first-rate bus and metro (subway) system, which is supplemented by funiculars, a new, if limited tramline and the historic Tramvia Blau, which climbs to the base of Tibidabo. Buses, the metro and the suburban railway, FGC, are fully integrated and tickets can be used on any of them for either one-system or combined journeys. Pick up a map of the network from a tourist information area or one of the TMB offices; these are in the metro stations at Plaça de la Universitat, Barcelona-Sants and Sagrada Familia.

● Information line ☎ 93 318 70 74 or 010

TICKETS

One-way tickets are available, but it makes sense to pay for multiple journeys using one of several types of *targeta* (travelcard):

● *Targeta* 10 (or T-10) valid for 10 trips by metro (and FGC) or bus.

● *Targeta* 30/50 valid for 50 trips within 30 days by metro (and FGC) or bus.

● You must cancel one unit of a *targeta* per journey undertaken by inserting it into the automatic machine at the entry to a station or aboard a bus. Changing from metro (or FGC) to bus or vice versa within 1 hour counts as one trip.

● Passes for unlimited bus and metro use are available for 1, 2, 3 and 5 days.

METRO

There are six metro lines, identified by number and colour. Direction is indicated by the name of the station at the end of the line.

● The network covers most parts of the city and is being extended ⓜ Mon–Thu and Sun 5am–midnight, Fri–Sat, and the evening before a public holiday 5am–2am, Sat 24 hours.

TRAINS

● Many main-line trains run beneath the city stopping at the underground stations at

Passeig de Gràcia and Plaça de Catalunya.
● Rail information: National ☎ 902 240 202

BUSES

Buses run 6.30am–10pm, though routes vary.
The free *Guía d'Autobusos Urbans de
Barcelona* details routes. As well as one-way
tickets, several types of *targeta* (travelcard) can
be used on the metro and buses.
● Targetas can only be bought at Metro sta-
tions, not onboard buses.
● More information (including frequency of
service) is given on the panels at bus stops.
● There is a night service, the *Nitbus*, with
routes around Plaça de Catalunya.
● Useful tourist routes include numbers 22
(Plaça de Catalunya-Gràcia-Tramvia Blau-
Pedralbes Monastery) and 24 (Plaça de
Catalunya-Gràcia-Parc Güell).

TAXI

● Black-and-yellow taxis can easily be hailed
on the street when displaying a green light
and the sign Lliure/Libre (free). There are large
taxi stands at the northern end of Las Ramblas
(opposite Plaça Catalunya) and at the southern end opposite the Columbus monument.
● Fares are not expensive, but a series of sup-
plements—for luggage, airport runs and past-
midnight rides—can bump up the fare.

ORGANIZED SIGHTSEEING

Easily the best buy in city sightseeing is the Bus
Turístic, which has three routes—one running
north of the city (red), one south and west
(blue) and a third eastward (green). One- and
two-day tickets entitle you to discounts on many
sights like the Poble Espanyol (▷ 34). Julià Tours
and Pullmantur offer half- and full-day bus tours
to principal sights. Tickets are sold at the Tourist
Information Centre in Plaça Catalunya and TMB
offices at Sants, Universitat and Sagrada Familia
metro stations. Various organizations provide
individual guides, who can give you a more personal introduction to Barcelona.

TAXI CONTACTS

If you need to call a taxi, try
these reputable services:
Radio Taxi
✉ 93 303 30 33
Servi Taxi
✉ 93 330 03 00
Taxi Groc
✉ 93 357 77 55
Taxi Class Rent
✉ 93 307 07 07
Taxi Miramar
✉ 93 433 10 20

TOURIST INFORMATION

✚ G7 ✉ Plaça Catalunya
s/n ⏱ Daily 9–9

✚ D5 ✉ Estació de Sants
⏱ Mon–Fri 8–8, Sat–Sun
8–2 (until 8 in summer)

✚ G8 ✉ Carrer Ciutat 2
(Ajuntament) ⏱ Mon–Fri
9–8, Sat 10–8, Sun 10–2

✚ G7 ✉ Las Ramblas 115
⏱ Daily 9–9

✚ G9 ✉ Portal de la Pau
s/n (in front of the Columbus
Monument) ⏱ Daily 9–9

✚ Off map ✉ El Prat
airport terminals A & B
⏱ Daily 9–9

Tourist Info phone line:
☎ 93 285 38 34

Essential Facts

TRAVELLER BEWARE

Be aware that, in certain areas of the city, petty crime rates are very high. Often thefts will occur using diversionary tactics to distract tourists' attention. The Raval area is particularly notorious after dark. Follow common-sense rules, such as carrying little cash and few credit cards, don't wear expensive jewellery, and leave passports and tickets in the hotel. If you are unfortunate enough to be a victim, you must report the theft to the police and be issued with the crime report in order to claim on your insurance.

USEFUL PHONE NUMBERS

- Police, fire and ambulance
☎ 112
- Nacional Police ☎ 091
- Local police ☎ 092
- General city information
☎ 010
- Turisme-Atenció (tourist assistance) ☎ 93 285 38 34

CUSTOMS REGULATIONS

- The limits for non-EU visitors are 200 cigarettes or 50 cigars, or 250g of tobacco; 1 litre of spirits (over 22 per cent) or 2 litres of fortified wine, 2 litres of still wine; 50g of perfume. The guidelines for EU residents (for personal use) are 800 cigarettes, or 200 cigars, or 1kg tobacco; 10 litres of spirits (over 22 per cent), 20 litres of aperitifs, or 90 litres of wine, of which 60 can be sparkling, or 110 litres of beer.
- Visitors under 17 are not entitled to the tobacco and alcohol allowances.

ELECTRICITY

- The standard current is 220/225 volts AC (sometimes 110/125 volts AC).
- Plugs are of round two-pin type. US visitors require an adaptor and a transformer.

OPENING HOURS

- Banks: Mon–Fri 8.30–2.
- Shops: Mon–Sat 9 or 10–1.30, 4.30–8 (hours vary). Larger shops/department stores may open all day. Some Sunday opening.
- Some small museums shut for lunch, close early on Sunday, and are shut all day Monday.
- Pharmacies (*Farmàcies*) offer a wider range of treatments and medicines than in many countries. Opening hours: Mon–Sat 9–1.30, 4.30–8.

HEALTH

- If you need a doctor, ask at your hotel as a first step. If you do not have private insurance you will only be entitled to see a doctor working within the Spanish State Health Service.
- Pharmacies are marked by a flashing green cross and operate a rota system so there is at least one open in every neighbourhood 24 hours a day. Farmàcia Alvarez, Passeig de Gràcia 26 and Farmàcia Clapés, La Rambla 98 are always open 24/7.

MONEY

● Credit cards are widely accepted in Barcelona and can be used in hotels, restaurants and shops. You will be asked to produce photo identification such as a passport or EU driving licence when using a credit card. Credit cards can also be used in automatic ticketing machines for the metro and RENFE lines.
● ATMs (*cajeros*) are found all over the city, with operating instructions in several languages, including English.

TOURIST CARDS AND SERVICES

Various *targetas* (cards) for tourists are available at the Tourist Information Offices (▷ 119) offering great discounts on the main sites and more.
● The Barcelona Card (cost €17–€36, valid for 1, 2 or 3 days) gives unlimited access to public transport and discounts at more than 100 museums, monuments, restaurants and shops.
● The Articket allows entry to the city's major museums and galleries; cost €20.
● The Arqueoticket offers entry to the city's five museums focused on archaeology and history; cost €17.
● Barcelona Turisme's walking tours are organized around themes, and offer great value as they always include at least one trip to a museum; cost approx €10.
● Barcelona Turisme is not the only place where tourists can gather information. The Centre d' Informació de la Virreina (✉ Las Ramblas 99 ☎ 93 301 7775) has brochures and information on the city's fiestas and cultural events, whilst the Palau Robert (✉ Passeig de Gràcia 107 ☎ 93 238 4000) has information on out-of-town destinations within Catalonia.

10 euros

50 euros

200 euros

500 euros

ETIQUETTE

● It's normal to wish people *bon dia*. Friends exchange kisses on both cheeks.
● Expect to find unabashed smokers in public places.
● Do not wear shorts or short skirts in churches.

CONSULATES	
Canada	✉ Elisenda de Pinós 10 ☎ 93 204 27 00
Ireland	✉ Gran Via Carles III 94 ☎ 93 491 50 21
United Kingdom	✉ Diagonal 477 ☎ 93 366 62 00
United States	✉ Passeig Reina Elisenda 23 ☎ 93 280 22 27

CHILDREN

● Children are welcome everywhere, and will be fussed over by everyone, but the standard and range of child-specific facilities do not approach those available in the UK or USA.

● Mother and baby-changing and feeding facilities are rare.

● Hotels will generally be happy to put an extra bed and/or cot in your room for an additional charge.

● Public transport is free for children under 4, but access to the metro with pushchairs (strollers) can be difficult.

● There are no menus specifically for kids, but most restaurants will happily serve children's portions.

● You will find children's play areas in parks and squares all over the city.

● Barcelona's beaches are clean, with play areas, showers and ice-cream kiosks.

● You can get a list of child-minding services from the tourist board.

TELEPHONES

● New public phones accept coins, phonecards, and credit cards. Phonecards are available from paper shops and newsstands.

● National operator ☎ 1009.

● International operator: Europe ☎ 1008; elsewhere ☎ 1005.

● Directory Enquiries: 11822; International 11825

● You must dial Barcelona's code (93), even within Barcelona.

● To phone the US from Spain, prefix the code and number with 001.

● To phone the UK from Spain, dial 00 44, then drop the first zero from the area code.

POST OFFICES

● Main post office (Correu Central)
🖂 Plaça Antoni López
☎ 93 486 80 50
🕐 Mon–Sat 8.30–10, Sun 9–2.30
🚇 Barceloneta

● Other post offices are at Aragó 282, Ronda Universitat 23 and Carrer València 231.

● Stamps are sold at paper shops and tobacconists.

● Mailboxes are yellow.

NEWSPAPERS

● International papers can be found on the newsstands on the Rambla and Passeig de Gràcia.

● The English-language monthly *Barcelona Metropolitan*, launched in 1996, has some listings and is free.

● The main current events periodical is the weekly *Guía del Ocio*.

● *ANUNTIS* is a free listings periodical.

Language

Catalan now enjoys equal status to Castillian Spanish in Barcelona and Catalonia, and must not be thought of as a dialect. Street signs and official communications are now exclusively in Catalan, but virtually everyone understands Castillian Spanish. Most people in the tourist industry speak some English and French. Any effort to speak Spanish or (especially) Catalan will be welcomed.

SOME SPANISH WORDS TO LOOK OUT FOR:

Spanish/Catalan

buenos días/bon dia	good morning
buenas tardes/ bona tarda	good evening
buenas noches/ bona nit	good night
hola/hola	hello
adiós/adéu	goodbye
gracias/gràcies	thank you
perdóne/perdoni	excuse me
de nada/de res	you're welcome
por favor/si us pla	please
si, no/sí, no	yes, no
abierto/obert	open
cerrado/tancat	closed
iglesia/església	church
palacio/palau	palace
museo/museu	museum
calle/carrer	street
aseos, servicios/ lavabo	restroom, toilet
lunes/dilluns	Monday
martes/dimarts	Tuesday
miércoles/dimecres	Wednesday
jueves/dijous	Thursday
viernes/divendres	Friday
sábado/dissabte	Saturday
domingo/diumenge	Sunday

CALLE OR CARRER

Barcelona's bi-lingualism needs to be understood when getting around. Both the Spanish *Calle* and Catalan *Carrer* are used to mean 'street' though this is mainly dropped in everyday conversation, thus Carrer or Calle de Pau Claris simply becomes 'Pau Claris.' Although by law all nomenclature must be in Catalan, people still use Spanish versions; compare Comerç (Catalan) to Comercio (Spanish) though this rarely causes more than a moment of confusion.

NUMBERS

Spanish/Catalan

un (uno/una), dos/un (una), dos	1, 2
tres, cuatro/ tres, quatre	3, 4
cinco, seis/ cinc, sis	5, 6
siete, ocho/ set, vuit	7, 8
nueve, diez/ nou, deu	9, 10

Timeline

BEFORE 1000

Barcelona's origins date back to 27BC–AD14, when the Romans founded Barcino during the reign of Emperor Augustus.

City walls were built in the late 3rd/early 4th century, as a result of attacks by Franks and Alemanni.

AD415 saw a Visigothic invasion and the establishment of the Kingdom of Tolosa, predecessor of Catalonia.

Arabs invaded in 717 and the city became Barjelunah. In 876 the Franks gained control.

FOR EIXAMPLE

In 1859, officials approved a plan for the Eixample, the grandiose extension of Barcelona beyond the city walls. The plan was finally developed in the late 19th and early 20th century, with many *modernista* buildings.

988 Catalonia becomes independent after the Franks decline to send support against the Moors.

1131–62 Ramon Berenguer IV reigns and the union of Catalonia and Aragon takes place. Barcelona becomes a major trading city.

1213–76 Jaume I reigns, and conquers Valencia, Ibiza and Mallorca from the Moors. New city walls are built.

1354 The legislative council of Catalonia—the Corts Catalans—sets up the Generalitat to control city finances.

1410 The last ruler of the House of Barcelona, Martí I, dies without an heir. Catalonia is now ruled from Madrid, which becomes more interested in transatlantic ventures than the trade of the Mediterranean.

1462–73 The Catalan civil war rages and the economy deteriorates.

1640 Els Segadors (the Reapers) revolt against Castilian rule.

1714 Barcelona is defeated by French and Spanish troops in the War of the Spanish Succession. Catalonia made Spanish province.

1813 Napoleonic troops depart. Textile manufacturing leads to a growth in the city's industry and population.

1888 The Universal Exhibition attracts 2 million visitors.

1909 Churches and convents are set aflame during the Setmana Tràgica (Tragic Week).

1914–18 Barcelona's economy is boosted by Spanish neutrality in World War I.

1931 The Catalan Republic is declared after the exile of King Alfonso XIII.

1939 Barcelona falls to the Nationalists, led by General Franco. Spain remains neutral during World War II.

1975 Franco dies. The restoration of the monarchy under Juan Carlos I allows the re-establishment of the Generalitat as the parliament of an autonomous regional government of Catalonia.

1992 Barcelona hosts the Olympic Games.

2002 *Any Internacional Gaudí* celebrates the 150th anniversary of Gaudí's birth.

2004 Barcelona hosts the UNESCO Universal Forum of Cultures.

2007 The Spanish Government recognizes Catalania as a 'nation' in the constitution.

FRANCO

In 1936, armed workers in Barcelona defeated an army uprising led by Nationalist General Franco. But resistance to Franco was weakened by internal strife between Communists and Anarchists. In 1939, Barcelona fell to the Nationalists. Catalan identity and culture were crushed during the subsequent Franco dictatorship. The Catalan language was banned and the region suffered economic decline. Franco died in 1975 and the monarchy was restored.

From left: A statue of St. George at the Generalitat, Philip V of Spain, the Monument à Colom, an old Barcelonan street, modernista buildings in the Ramblas, General Franco

Index

Barcelona's
25 BEST

WRITTEN BY Michael Ivory
ADDITIONAL WRITING Sally Roy
UPDATED BY Suzanne Wales
DESIGN WORK Jacqueline Bailey
COVER DESIGN Tigist Getachew
INDEXER Marie Lorimer
IMAGE RETOUCHING AND REPRO Michael Moody and Sarah Montgomery
REVIEWING EDITOR Paul Eisenberg
SERIES EDITOR Marie-Claire Jefferies

ISBN 978-1-4000-0798-1

FIFTH EDITION

IMPORTANT TIP
Time inevitably brings changes, so always confirm prices, travel facts, and other perishable information when it matters. Although Fodor's cannot accept responsibility for errors, you can use this guide in the confidence that we have taken every care to ensure its accuracy.

SPECIAL SALES
This book is available for special discounts for bulk purchases for sales promotions or premiums. Special editions, including personalized covers, excerpts of existing books, and corporate imprints, can be created in large quantities for special needs. For more information, write to Special Markets/Premium Sales, 1745 Broadway, MD 6–2, New York, NY 10019 or email specialmarkets@randomhouse.com.

Color separation by Keenes, Andover, UK
Printed and bound by Leo Paper Products, China
10 9 8 7 6 5 4 3 2

A04245
Maps in this title produced from mapping © MAIRDUMONT / Falk Verlag 2009
Transport map © Communicarta Ltd, UK

The Automobile Association would like to thank the following photographers, companies and picture libraries for their assistance in the preparation of this book.

Abbreviations for the picture credits are as follows: - (t) top; (b) bottom; (l) left; (r) right: (AA) AA World Travel Library.

1 AA/S L Day; **2** AA/M Jourdan; **3** AA/M Jourdan; **4t** AA/M Jourdan; **4l** AA/S L Day; **5t** AA/M Jourdan; **5** AA/S L Day; **6t** AA/M Jourdan; **6cl** AA/M Jourdan; **6c** AA/M Chaplow; **6cr** AA/S L Day; **6bl** AA/M Chaplow; **6bc** A/M Chaplow; **6br** AA/M Chaplow; **7t** AA/M Jourdan; **7cl** AA/S L Day; **7c** AA/S L Day; **7cr** AA/M Jourdan; **7bl** AA/M Chaplow; **7bc** AA/M Chaplow; **7br** AA/S L Day; **8t** AA/M Jourdan; **9t** AA/M Jourdan; **10t** AA/M Jourdan; **10tr** AA/S McBride; **10ctr** AA/S McBride; **10cbr** AA/S McBride; **10br** AA/M Chaplow; **11t** AA/M Jourdan; **11tl** AA/S McBride; **11ctl** AA/S McBride; **11cbl** AA/S McBride; **11bl** AA/S McBride; **12t** AA/M Jourdan; **12bl** AA/M Chaplow; **13t** AA/M Jourdan; **13tl** AA/M Jourdan; **13ctl** AA/S McBride; **13cl** Digital Vision; **13cbl** Photodisc; **13bl** Brand X Pictures; **14t** AA/M Jourdan; **14tr** AA/M McBride; **14ctr** AA/S McBride; **14cbr** AA/S McBride; **14br** AA/S McBride; **15t** AA/M Jourdan; **15br** AA/S McBride; **16t** AA/M Jourdan; **16tr** AA/S McBride; **16cr** AA/S McBride; **16br** AA/S L Day; **17t** AA/M Jourdan; **17tl** AA/S L Day; **17ctl** AA/S L Day; **17cbl** AA/M Chaplow; **17bl** A/S McBride; **18t** AA/M Jourdan; **18tr** AA/S L Day; **18ctr** AA/M Chaplow; **18cbr** AA/S L Day; **18br** AA/M Jourdan; **19t** AA/S L Day; **19ct** AA/M Jourdan; **19c** AA/M Jourdan; **19cb** AA/M Jourdan; **19b** AA/M Chaplow; **20/1** AA/M Chaplow; **24/5** AA/M Jourdan; **25tr** AA/M Jourdan; **25cr** AA/P Wilson; **26/7** AA/S L Day, (©Successió Miró/ ADAGP, Paris and DACS, London 2006); **27** AA/P Wilson, (©Successió Miró/ADAGP, Paris and DACS, London 2006); **28** AA/M Jourdan; **28/9** AA/M Jourdan; **29** AA/M Jourdan; **30l** AA/S L Day; **30r** AA/S L Day; **31t** AA/S L Day; **31b** AA/M Jourdan; **32** AA/M Chaplow; **32/3** AA/M Jourdan; **34t** AA/S L Day; **34bl** AA/M Jourdan; **34br** AA/P Wilson; **35t** AA/C Sawyer; **36t** AA/S McBride; **36c** AA/M Jourdan; **37t** Digital Vision; **38t** AA/S McBride; **39** AA/S L Day; **42l** AA/S L Day; **42/3t** AA/S L Day; **42/3c** AA/S L Day; **43tr** AA/M Jourdan; **43cr** AA/M Jourdan; **44** AA/M Jourdan; **44/5t** AA/M Chaplow; **44/5c** AA/S L Day; **45** AA/M Jourdan; **46** AA/M Jourdan; **46/7** AA/S L Day; **48l** AA/S L Day; **48c** AA/P Wilson; **48r** AA/M Chaplow; **49l** AA/S McBride; **49r** AA/S McBride; **50t** AA/S L Day; **50bl** AA/M Chaplow; **50br** AA/P Wilson; **51t** AA/S L Day; **51b** AA/S L Day; **52** AA/C Sawyer; **53t** AA/S McBride; **54t** AA/M Chaplow; **55t** Digital Vision; **56** AA/M Jourdan; **57t** AA/S McBride; **58t** AA/S McBride; **59** Ricard Pla and Pere Vivas/Palau de la Música Catalana; **62l** AA/M Jourdan; **62r** AA/M Jourdan; **63l** AA/M Chaplow; **63c** AA/M Chaplow; **63r** Las Meninas, No. 30, 1957, (oil on canvas), Picasso, Pablo (1881-1973)/Museu Picasso, Barcelona, Spain, Giraudon/The Bridgeman Art Library/© Succession Picasso/DACS 2006; **64l** AA/M Jourdan; **64r** Ricard Pla and Pere Vivas/Palau de la Música Catalana; **65l** AA/M Chaplow; **65c** AA/M Jourdan; **65r** AA/M Jourdan; **66l** AA/S L Day; **66r** AA/P Wilson; **67l** AA/M Chaplow; **67r** AA/M Chaplow; **68l** AA/M Jourdan; **68/9t** AA/S L Day; **69cr** AA/M Jourdan; **69cl** AA/M Jourdan; **69r** AA/M Jourdan; **70l** AA/M Jourdan; **70/1** AA/P Wilson; **71** AA/S L Day; **72t** AA/S L Day; **72bl** AA/M Jourdan; **72br** AA/M Jourdan; **73** AA/C Sawyer; **74t** AA/S McBride; **75t** AA/S McBride; **76t** Photodisc; **77t** AA/C Sawyer; **78t** AA/S McBride; **78br** AA/C Sawyer; **79** AA/S L Day; **82** AA/S L Day; **83l** AA/M Jourdan; **83r** AA/M Chaplow; **84** AA/S L Day; **84/5** AA/S L Day; **85t** AA/M Chaplow; **85cl** AA/S L Day; **85cr** AA/M Jourdan; **86l** AA/P Wilson; **86/7** AA/S L Day; **86cr** AA/S L Day; **87r** AA/M Jourdan; **87c** AA/M Chaplow; **88** AA/S L Day; **88/9t** AA/M Jourdan; **88/9c** AA/M Jourdan; **89** AA/M Jourdan; **90** AA/S L Day; **90/1** AA/M Jourdan; **91** AA/S L Day; **92t** AA/S L Day; **92bl** AA/M Jourdan; **92br** AA/M Chaplow; **93t** AA/C Sawyer; **93r** AA/M Chaplow; **94t** AA/M Chaplow; **95t** AA/S McBride; **96t** Digital Vision; **97t** AA/S McBride; **98t** AA/C Sawyer; **99** AA/S L Day; **102/3t** AA/M Jourdan; **102cl** AA/M Jourdan; **102/3c** AA/S L Day; **103** AA/M Jourdan; **104l** AA/P Enticknap; **104r** AA/S L Day; **105t** AA/S L Day; **105b** AA/M Chaplow; **106t** AA/S L Day; **106bl** LH Images/Alamy; **106br** AA/S L Day; **107** AA/S McBride; **108t** AA/C Sawyer; **108tr** AA/S McBride; **108ctr** AA/S McBride; **108cbr** AA/C Sawyer; **108br** AA/M Chaplow; **109t/112t** AA/C Sawyer; **113** AA/S L Day; **114t/117t** AA/S McBride; **118t/120t** AA/S McBride; **120l** AA/M Jourdan; **121t** AA/S McBride; **121r** European Central Bank; **122t/123t** AA/S McBride; **122l** AA/M Chaplow; **122r** AA/M Chaplow; **124t** AA/S McBride; **124bl** AA/P Wilson; **124bc** AA; 124br AA/P Wilson; **124/5b** AA; **125t** AA/S McBride; **125bc** AA/M Jourdan; **125br** Illustrated London News.

Every effort has been made to trace the copyright holders, and we apologise in advance for an unintentional omissions or errors. We would be please to apply any corrections to any following edition of this publication.